THE ADVENT OF TIME

THE ADVENT
OF TIME

*A Solution to the Problem of Evil Based on the
Prerequisites of Love & an Analysis of Timeless Being*

Indignus Servus

Ex-Voto Publishing, LLC
Chapel Hill, North Carolina
United States of America

BISAC Subject Heading:
RELIGION / Christian Theology / Apologetics (REL067030)

Library of Congress Control Number:
2024901683

ISBNs:
979-8-9899166-2-7 (Hardcover)
979-8-9899166-1-0 (Paperback)
979-8-9899166-0-3 (eBook, Kindle Edition)

CONTENTS

INTRODUCTION

The theological problem posed by the existence of evil and suffering is arguably the longest-standing and most potent challenge to monotheistic belief. Contemporary authors often present this problem in the form of a logic game, expressed by a series of three propositions that appear to be logically contradictory:

(1) God is all-powerful (i.e., omnipotent);

(2) God is all-loving (i.e., omnibenevolent);

(3) Evil and suffering exist.

If God is all-loving then he would certainly want to spare his creatures from evil. If God is all-powerful then he should be able to remove evil, or at least prevent his creatures from suffering. Yet evil and suffering not only exist, the world is inundated with them. Why?

This seemingly unanswerable question has been called "the rock of atheism,"[1] and for good reason—it has prompted the deconversion of untold numbers of believers, including many Christian scholars, theologians, and clergy. Among them is John Loftus, a former Christian preacher who renounced his faith after concluding that the problem of evil cannot be solved.[2] In his 2008 book, *Why I Became an Atheist,* Loftus quotes his former classmate from divinity school, Dr. James Sennett, on the importance religious scholars place on the problem of evil: "By far the most important objection to the faith is the so-called problem of evil—the alleged incompatibility between the existence or extent of evil in the world and the existence of God. I tell my philosophy of religion students that, if they are Christians and the problem of evil does not keep them up at night, then they don't understand it."[3]

There are several reasons why many Christians fail to appreciate the gravity and enormity of the problem of evil, including confusion over the precise meaning of the word "evil." More than 1,500 years ago, Saint Augustine described evil as the "privation of good" in his seminal work, *The City of God*.[4] Since then, a significant portion of the debate over the problem of evil has focused on Augustine's arguments, but his definition of evil has been criticized for its tendency to minimize the seriousness of evil. After all, to define evil as the absence of good is to suggest a kind of "nothingness" in its place, not the presence of something affirmatively wicked or wrong.

In contrast, the word "pain" has a tangible, real-world meaning that is readily understood by everyone acquainted with life. Unlike the concept of evil, which can be defined in various ways, the concept of pain is straightforward. It describes experiences of actual hurt—sometimes brutal and ghastly—that everyone has known, felt, and endured. The problem of pain is a real-life problem, not something removed and distant that concerns only academics and philosophers. For this reason, and because the existence of both "pain" and "evil" raise the same basic theological difficulty even though they refer to distinct concepts, the phrase "problem of pain" is emphasized over "problem of evil" in the discussion that follows.[5]

A second and more common reason many people fail to understand the seriousness of the problem of pain is a false belief

that a comprehensive solution has been provided by the so-called
"free will argument." According to this view, the reason there is
so much suffering in the world is because God has given humans
free will. Without the free will to obey and love God, man would
be nothing more than an automaton. True free will implies the
ability to love and obey, as well as the ability to hate and disobey.
When humanity chooses the latter over the former, suffering is
the result.

Suffering that results from corruption, theft, war, and other
such social or political ills can be fairly attributed to humanity's
misuse of free will, in many if not all cases. But what about suffering that is caused by other sources, such as disease and natural
disasters? As the religious scholar Dr. Bart Ehrman points out, the
causes of human suffering are tremendously varied, and many of
these causes appear to be largely or entirely unrelated to human
decision-making: "Yes, you can explain the political machinations
of competing political forces in Ethiopia (or in Nazi Germany
or in Stalin's Soviet Union or in the ancient worlds of Israel and
Mesopotamia) by claiming that human beings had badly handled
the freedom given to them. But how can you explain drought?
When it hits, it is not because someone chose not to make it rain.
Or how do you explain a hurricane that destroys New Orleans? Or
a tsunami that kills hundreds of thousands overnight? Or earth-
quakes, or mudslides, or malaria, or dysentery? The list goes on."[6]

In response to the observation that the problem of pain
cannot be fully answered through the free will argument, some
thinkers have reasoned that man's experience of suffering can
be explained on the grounds that it serves as a mechanism to
promote spiritual growth and positive character development.
John Hick advocates for this position in *Evil and the God of Love*:

Antitheistic writers almost invariably assume a conception of the divine purpose which is contrary to the Christian conception. They assume that the purpose of a loving God must be to create a hedonistic paradise; and therefore to the extent that the world is other than this, it proves to them that God is either not loving enough or not powerful enough to create such a world...

Certainly we seek pleasure for our children, and take great delight in obtaining it for them; but we do not desire for them unalloyed pleasure at the expense of their growth in such even greater values as moral integrity, unselfishness, compassion, courage, humor, reverence for the truth, and perhaps above all the capacity for love...

If, then, there is any true analogy between God's purpose for his human creatures, and the purpose of loving and wise parents for their children, we have to recognize that the presence of pleasure and the absence of pain cannot be the supreme and overriding end for which the world exists. Rather, this world must be a place of soul-making.[7]

Hick makes a reasonable case, but what about pain that neither enables some type of positive spiritual growth or character development, nor is the consequence of someone's misuse of free will? Consider the following example: an infant enters the world crippled and sickly. His childhood is spent bedridden and wheelchair-bound, battling one illness after the next, slowly exhausting his mental and emotional strength. By the time he reaches adolescence, he is psychologically and spiritually broken and decides to take his own life.

In this example, the experience of suffering did not serve to strengthen the moral resolve of the child. Instead, the child's suffering gradually but relentlessly wore down his will to live, eventually overwhelming it. The result of this brutal, grinding experience of suffering was the creation of a being so thoroughly demoralized that he decided to commit suicide.

Sadly, this cruel example of suffering is not a hypothetical scenario; it is a case drawn from real life. Even worse, it is but one of countless real-world examples of people who have been driven to suicide or insanity because of suffering. One could argue that such broken individuals serve the greater good of allowing others to act compassionately toward them, but this is tantamount to saying that the most unfortunate members of the human race exist only to manure the spiritual growth of others.

For many, such a notion is difficult to reconcile with the existence of an all-loving and all-powerful God. Nonetheless, since at least some potential benefit can be identified that stems from these instances of suffering, one cannot entirely dismiss the idea that a certain amount of man's suffering may exist for the purpose of facilitating the spiritual growth of others.

But even if it could be credibly claimed that a significant portion of human suffering exists for the purpose of furthering the spiritual growth of others, innumerable instances of suffering exist that appear to be entirely pointless, such as the following hypothetical example: a lone hiker is walking through a remote forest when a random gust of wind suddenly causes a tree to fall on him, crushing his torso and trapping him. The hiker is badly injured and delirious from pain, but no one is aware he is lying in the forest, dying an agonizing death over the course of a day's time. In this example, what greater good does the hiker or anyone else gain from his dreadful experience of suffering?

The explanation provided by John Hick fails to answer this question because the hiker is unable to gain any character-building or spirit-building benefit in his delirious, pain-racked state. Because no one else is aware of the incident, there is no one to help the hiker, nor is there anyone who knows enough about the hiker's predicament to even feel compassion for him. Since the immediate cause of this suffering was a random natural event, not the misuse of someone's free will, it would appear to be absolutely pointless. If there really is an all-loving and all-powerful God, why does he permit such instances of apparently useless suffering?

The existence of vast amounts of seemingly gratuitous suffering is a problem that has never been satisfactorily addressed by the litany of popular and academic responses to the problem of pain that have been advanced over the centuries. In the absence of a comprehensive explanation to justify the immense misery and suffering that takes place in this world, many serious thinkers have become convinced that the "rock of atheism" is impregnable. If the problem of pain were indeed capable of being solved, they argue, it surely would have been by now.[8]

But with theists unable to offer anything more than partial answers to explain why an omnipotent and omnibenevolent God would allow the occurrence of the enormously varied forms of suffering experienced by both humans and other creatures, the problem of pain has remained a singularly powerful argument against belief in the existence of the Christian God. As explained by Dr. A. M. Weisberger, a professor of philosophy who delivers an incisive critique of theodicy in *Suffering Belief: Evil and the Anglo-American Defense of Theism*, the failure to provide a truly comprehensive answer to the problem of evil is a failure that casts doubt on the credibility of core Christian assertions regarding the nature and character of God: "Any proposed solution to the problem of evil which does not account for all kinds of evil in the world, both moral and natural, is deficient in some way, since evil is then not shown to be necessary. And if some evil is not necessary, God's goodness and/or power is called into question."[9] If God's goodness or power is called into question, Christianity itself is too.

The Advent of Time provides a comprehensive solution to the most confounding enigma of the Christian faith, one based on insights not found in other theodicies. The key features that distinguish this book from other works on this subject are the following:

(1)   The assertion that love is the principal end for which God allows suffering (as opposed to free will, character development, or one of the various other objectives that have been put forth in previous theodicies).

(2)   The identification of five prerequisites of love.

(3)   An explanation of why these prerequisites of love—together with the limits that God places on the exercise of his absolute power by virtue of his perfectly loving, perfectly just, and perfectly wise nature—necessitate that God allow for the possibility of evil and suffering if humanity is to have the opportunity to experience timeless love with God and one another.

(4)   An analysis and interpretation of Genesis 1–3 based on concepts of time and being that have been raised in theological works describing man's final state of existence.

7

While the focus on these four areas represents a departure from traditional approaches to solving the problem of evil, it is important to note that the arguments in this book still strictly adhere to all core aspects of Christian orthodoxy. As the *Catechism of the Catholic Church* so aptly asserts, *"There is not a single aspect of the Christian message that is not in part an answer to the question of evil."*[10] Because of this, at various points in the pages that follow, it is necessary to provide an overview of certain foundational Christian precepts.

The discussion of these precepts draws upon insight and analysis from an array of Christian thinkers, but readers are advised that the arguments below align most closely with the theology of the Catholic Church.[11] The principal Catholic reference that is relied upon is the *Catechism of the Catholic Church*, which has been declared by Catholic ecclesiastical leadership to be a "sure norm for teaching the faith."[12] The *Catechism* is a frequently cited reference because it captures in a single authoritative source widely held foundational Christian doctrine on a range of relevant topics.

Some readers may already have intricate knowledge of these doctrines. Others may have little to no familiarity with them. No book on a subject as complex as the problem of evil can be written in a manner that perfectly suits all groups. This book assumes that readers are generally acquainted with the most well-known beliefs that the majority of Christians hold in common with one another, but it does not assume that readers have explored the nuances of these beliefs.

Finally, even though the intended audience is not Christian clergy or scholars, this book assumes that readers are willing and able to think through the implications of basic theological arguments that rest upon Christian tenets. The purpose of these arguments is not to offer emotional or pastoral support to those who are suffering. Rather, the purpose of this book is to provide a comprehensive but concise answer to the problem of evil that aligns with Christian orthodoxy, without violating any formal rule of logic or denying the well-established findings of natural science.

PART I: REDEFINING AN ANCIENT PROBLEM

The Greek Stoic philosopher Epicurus (341 BC–270 BC) is frequently credited as being the first to articulate the problem of pain as a three-part problem, consisting of a conflict between the following assertions:

(1)   God is all-powerful;

(2)   God is all-loving;

(3)   Pain and suffering exist.[13]

During the more than two millennia that have elapsed since this version of the problem of pain was formulated, most prominent theodicies have remained focused on the narrow set of assertions listed by Epicurus. Even Christian theists have largely seemed content to confine their arguments to the limits established by this pre-Christian framework, despite the fact that the Bible identifies a number of other vitally important characteristics of God.

To understand the solution to the problem of pain, it is necessary to part with excessively restrictive conceptions of God. This requires redefining the problem of pain to take into account the following four divine attributes: God is all-powerful, God is all-loving, God is all-just, and God is all-wise.[14] In addition, it is assumed that God, in his wisdom, prioritizes love over other considerations. Biblical support for this assumption appears throughout the New Testament but perhaps most powerfully in Matthew 22:34–40, when Christ tells the Pharisees that the greatest of all God's commandments is the commandment to love:

> When the Pharisees heard that he had silenced the Sadducees, they gathered together, and one of them, a lawyer, asked him a question to test him. "Teacher, which commandment in the law is the greatest?" He said to him, "'You shall love the Lord your God with all your heart, and with all your soul, and with all your mind.' This is the greatest and first commandment. And the second is like it: 'You shall love your neighbor as yourself.' On these two commandments hang all the law and the prophets."[15]

Applying the additional factors outlined above, the new problem set is as follows:

(1) God is all-powerful;

(2) God is all-loving;

(3) God is all-just;

(4)   God is all-wise, and in his wisdom, God ranks love
       before justice;

(5)   Creation is filled with immense evil, pain, and
       suffering.

This broader accounting of God's attributes and character
traits will allow the problem of pain to be examined in a different
light. But before the problem of pain can be answered using this
five-part paradigm, the first four assertions must be analyzed in
greater detail. This analysis will provide foundational concepts
that will be relied upon in Part II to provide a comprehensive
solution to the problem of pain.

GOD IS ALL-POWERFUL

The problem of pain centers on the argument that it is contradictory to assert that God is omnipotent yet is somehow impeded from putting an end to suffering. In order to address this argument, it is necessary to begin by identifying two ways in which God's power may appear limited when in fact it is not.

First, any character trait of God represents a constraint God voluntarily imposes on the exercise of his absolute power. For example, to assert that God is both omnipotent and all-loving is to simultaneously assert that God never chooses to use his absolute power in an unloving manner. If, in addition to being all-loving, God is also all-just and all-wise, it follows that God will not exercise his absolute power in a manner that is unjust or unwise. The assertions "God is all-loving," "God is all-just," and "God is all-wise" can therefore be viewed as three distinct restraints God imposes on the use of his absolute power.

It is important to understand that these restraints in no way imply that God is anything less than completely omnipotent. The assertion "God is all-powerful" means God has the ability to do anything that is not a logical contradiction.[16] Consequently, absolute power includes the ability to be hateful, imprudent, and unfair. To assert that God is all-powerful but is also all-loving, all-just, and all-wise is to declare that God voluntarily exercises his omnipotence only in certain ways. God has the power to be hateful, but he chooses to act in a benevolent manner instead; God has the power to act imprudently, but he always chooses to act wisely; God has the power to be unjust, but he consistently chooses not to exercise his power in an unjust manner.

To gain a better understanding of why these voluntary restraints on the use of power do not constitute a lack of absolute power itself, consider how people consistently refrain from exercising certain powers that they possess. Each person reading this book has the power to commit suicide, but no one reading this book has chosen to exercise this power. The fact that no one reading these words has chosen to exercise the power to take his own life does not negate his ability to do so. The power to end one's life exists regardless of whether an individual ever chooses to exercise it.

To answer the problem of pain, it is crucial to recognize the distinction between the ability to carry out a particular act (the existence of a power) and the choice of whether to actually carry out that act (the exercise of a power). A repeated, consistent choice not to exercise a certain power is the basis of a character trait. If a man chooses not to lie or be deceitful, he has a character for truthfulness. An individual's refusal to be dishonest in no way means he lacks the ability to be dishonest. Likewise, God's voluntary adherence to a set of strict behavioral standards does not constitute a lack of absolute power; it is simply a choice about how to exercise absolute power. God's perfect adherence to such behavioral standards is perhaps the most obvious manner in which his power may appear limited even though it is not.

A second way God's power can appear to be circumscribed is if he gives some of it away, either temporarily or permanently.[17] For instance, God has the ability to create other living beings, vest those living beings with a portion of God's power, and then refrain from taking that power back.[18] In effect, a power transfer occurs each time God creates a living being and imbues it with its own free will. Every time God creates such a being, God voluntarily diminishes his own power by the same degree to which he vests a creature with power to act independently.[19]

It may be helpful to think of this notion as the "law of conservation of power," to borrow a phrase from the field of physics. God has control over all power that exists, but God can hand over portions of this power to other living creatures at his discretion. When God transfers a portion of his power to beings that he creates, he relinquishes control over that power. In her essay, *Forms of the Implicit Love of God*, Simone Weil describes this concept as follows:

> On God's part creation is not an act of self-expansion but of restraint and renunciation... He emptied a part of his being from himself... God permitted the existence of things distinct from himself and worth infinitely less than himself. By this creative act he denied himself, as Christ has told us to deny ourselves. God denied himself for our sakes in order to give us the possibility of denying ourselves for him. This response, this echo, which is in our power to refuse, is the only possible justification for the folly of love of the creative act.
>
> The religions which have a conception of this renunciation, this voluntary distance, this voluntary effacement of God, his apparent absence and his secret presence here below, these religions are true religion, the translation into different languages of the great Revelation. The religions which

represent divinity as commanding wherever it has
the power to do so seem false.[20]

Assuming Weil's description is accurate, why would an omniscient and omnibenevolent God refrain from "commanding
wherever it has the power to do so," knowing that one of the
consequences of this decision is to permit the existence of pain?
Weil asserts that it is "in order to give us the possibility of denying
ourselves for him," but this hardly seems like a sufficient reason
considering the magnitude of pain and suffering in existence.

As it turns out, the selflessness entailed in "denying ourselves
for him" is a prerequisite of a profoundly more important reason
God chose to "empty a part of his being from himself." This reason
is the subject of the next chapter.

GOD IS ALL-LOVING

Love Is the Purpose of Human Creation

In order to answer the problem of pain, it is necessary to identify the primary purpose for which God created humanity. With respect to this issue, it is assumed God created humanity for the sake of allowing God and man to experience love with one another. This assumption stands at the very center of Christian doctrine and belief,[21] and it is stated unambiguously by Jesus himself in Matthew 22:34–40 and Mark 12:28–34 when he teaches that the greatest commandment is to love God, and the second greatest commandment is to love one another.

This teaching is known as the "Great Commandment" because every other God-given commandment and directive in the entire Bible, without exception, is subordinate to it and leads to it in some way or another.[22] The person who does not grasp the pivotal, overriding importance of love in Christianity has missed that which is most essential about the world's largest religion.[23] As First John 4:8 declares, "He who does not love does not know God; for God is love."[24]

Of course, if love is in fact the principal purpose of human existence, then this central precept of Christianity should make sense not only as an abstract theological concept; it should also align with man's real-world lived experience.

If one focuses attention exclusively on the pain and suffering man experiences during the course of his life, it is easy to conclude man's life experiences provide little if any support to the notion that love is the principal purpose of human existence. But before settling on this conclusion, consider the issue in light of the following two points. First, if God exists and is indeed an all-loving being, it stands to reason that man's happiness is of immense concern to him. Second, if God created humanity for some central, overriding purpose, then it is reasonable to assume that man's experience of this purpose will coincide with his greatest experiences of happiness. Stated plainly, a rational, all-loving, all-powerful God would not create man for a purpose that conflicts with that which brings man the greatest happiness.

Since its inception in the 1800s, the field of psychology has mostly focused its attention on the study of psychological pathologies and other forms of mental illness. However, in recent decades, increasing numbers of researchers have turned their attention to the study of human happiness, leading to the production of a sizable body of peer-reviewed scientific studies on the sources of happiness. One of the recurring findings of these studies is that, more than any other factor, human happiness is contingent on friendship and love.

In a 2002 study of 222 undergraduate students, researchers compared the upper 10 percent of consistently "very happy" participants in the study against participants who self-reported an average level of happiness, as well as those who self-reported significant unhappiness. The researchers discovered that the "very happy people were highly social, and had stronger romantic and other social relationships than less happy groups."[25] A 2018 study found that individuals who pursued happiness through social means, which entailed expending time and effort developing and maintaining relationships with others, reported higher levels of life satisfaction than those who pursued happiness through non-social means.[26]

Another study published in 2018 determined that people who offer the highest levels of emotional support to others are likely to be happier than individuals who are less compassionate.[27] Studies in 2006 and 2010 examining happiness among middle-aged and geriatric populations concluded that strong marriages and friendships are the best predictors of life satisfaction and day-to-day happiness in these groups.[28] A 2018 study of the "role of friends" in life satisfaction showed that "friendship, in terms of intensity (measured by the frequency with which individuals see their friends) and quality (measured by the satisfaction with friendship relationships), is positively associated to life satisfaction."[29]

Just as study after study has found a strong correlation between the strength of individuals' friendships and their level of happiness, study after study has found that individuals who have weak friendships, as well as individuals who experience significant loneliness and social disconnectedness, suffer from the highest levels of unhappiness and depression.[30] Similar findings have emerged from research into the effects of forcibly imposed social isolation. Specifically, researchers have found that inmates who are placed into solitary confinement for extended periods of time experience higher levels of psychological distress than inmates who have regular social interaction.[31]

These and numerous other academic studies clearly establish the importance of friendship and love to human happiness.[32] But what does research say about the relationship between happiness and the attainment of status-oriented goals, like wealth and reputation? It is a commonly held belief that increased wealth and social prominence bring greater happiness, but is this belief supported by the findings of peer-reviewed scientific research?

In 2009, researchers surveyed recent college graduates and compared their level of happiness against the type of goals they set for themselves. Those with "intrinsic" goals, like developing strong relationships, were significantly happier than those who pursued "extrinsic" goals, such as achieving wealth or reputation. The group that pursued extrinsic goals also suffered more negative emotions, like fear and shame, and experienced more physical ailments than the group that pursued intrinsic goals.[33] A 2010 study revealed that once individuals achieve close to the median level of income in their society, money ceases to increase their emotional well-being.[34]

If wealth and status are less important than friends to the attainment of happiness, what about other hedonistic ends[35] that are often pursued as a means to achieving happiness, such as the experience of sexual encounters with a variety of different romantic partners? Specifically, does having sex with more people lead to greater happiness?

A 2004 study examined the "links between income, sexual behavior and reported happiness…using data on a sample of 16,000 adult Americans."[36] This research found: "Sexual activity enters strongly positively in happiness equations. Higher income does not buy more sex or more sexual partners. Married people have more sex than those who are single, divorced, widowed or separated. The happiness-maximizing number of sexual partners in the previous year is calculated to be 1."

Taken together, the body of scientific research on human happiness provides compelling evidence that the most important source of happiness is the existence of close social ties—specifically, the presence of strong and enduring loving relationships with friends and family, as well as intimate and committed spousal relationships.[37] Though many other factors also impact individuals' sense of well-being and life satisfaction, studies reveal that friendship and love are unmatched in providing people with happiness. Studies have also found the reverse to be true; human beings are significantly more prone to psychological problems, particularly depression, when intimate connections to others are lacking.

These findings are supported by the longest-ever study of human well-being, Harvard's "Study of Adult Development." It commenced in the late 1930s when a group of Harvard University researchers began following the lives of two groups of men "to identify the psychosocial predictors of healthy aging."[38] The first group, known as the "Grant Study," was composed of 268 Harvard graduates from the classes of 1939–1944. The second group, the "Glueck Study," was made up of 456 men who grew up in the inner-city neighborhoods of Boston.[39]

Over the more than eight decades of this study, the well-being of the study's participants was assessed on a recurring basis, with the goal of discovering the causes of differences that emerged in their mental and physical health as they grew older and their lives took divergent paths. Through regular medical examinations, psychological assessments, interviews, and questionnaires, researchers tracked the study participants through their young adult years in Cambridge and Boston and continued tracking them through their active-duty military experiences in World War II, through marriages and divorces, career advancement and decline, retirement, and advanced age. The personal lives and professional careers of the study participants varied widely and included men who fell into addiction and ruin, as well as individuals who experienced spectacular professional success, including one who became president of the United States.[40]

Speaking in 2017, Robert Waldinger, director of the Study of Adult Development, described the central outcome of the research as follows: "The clearest message that we get from this 75-year study is this: Good relationships keep us happier and healthier. Period."[41]

Harvard psychiatrist George Vaillant, lead researcher of the Grant portion of the study for forty-two years, provided a similar description of the study's main findings. In a 2008 newsletter addressed to the subjects of the study and their families, Vaillant responded to the question, "What have you learned from the Grant Study men?" His reply: "That the only thing that really matters in life are your relationships to other people."[42] Four years later, Vaillant published *Triumphs of Experience: The Men of the Harvard Grant Study,* in which he uses examples from the lives of specific participants in the study to highlight key findings and conclusions from the research.[43] His chief takeaway from a career spent following the lives of the men of the Grant Study is this: "Happiness is love. Full stop."[44]

Formal studies aside, it is a common anecdotal observation that the happiest people in this world are not those with the most money, power, fame, or sexual partners, but rather those who are able to enjoy the strongest, most genuine friendships with other people, irrespective of wealth or social rank. This observation has been made by respected thinkers for millennia. In *Nicomachean Ethics,* Aristotle wrote, "Without friends no one would choose to live, though he had all other goods."[45]

Such observations raise an important question: if friendship and love are the wellsprings of human happiness, is it possible mankind was specifically designed for the purpose of experiencing friendship and love?

The Prerequisites of Relational Love

If there is merit to the idea that mankind was designed for the purpose of experiencing friendship and love then it is appropriate to ask, what is a friend?

The Bible is rich with descriptions of friendship, the book of Proverbs especially so. Proverbs 17:17 says, "A friend loves at all times."[46] Proverbs 18:24 declares that a true friend can be relied upon even more than a brother.[47] Proverbs 27:6 asserts that a friend only wounds in ways that are trustworthy and beneficial: "Faithful are the wounds of a friend."[48] John 15:13 explains that friends sacrifice for the benefit of one another.[49]

Summarizing the lessons of these verses, as well as the lessons of everyday experience, a reasonable case can be made that at least five elements must be present in order for friendship or relational love (as opposed to unrequited love) to be experienced:

(1)   Two (or more) persons;

(2)   Both (or all) of whom possess the power to affect one another through their actions;

(3)   Each must voluntarily;

(4)   Place faith in one another to treat each other in a beneficent manner; and

(5)   Act selflessly toward one another. This final requirement includes affirmative acts of kindness, as well as abstention from the pursuit of self-centered ends that can only be obtained at the expense of the other person. Both of these forms of selflessness require at least some level of self-sacrifice.

When each of these prerequisites is considered in turn, it can be seen that the absence of even a single one precludes the experience of relational love.

Starting with the first and most obvious element, it is easy to understand why relational love cannot be experienced without the existence of at least two individuals. If only a single person inhabited Earth, and there were no other beings with whom this person could interact, there would be no opportunity for this person to experience friendship or relational love. Loving relationships are not something an individual experiences by himself. It is self-evident that friendship, by its very nature, cannot occur without the existence of two or more persons.

Now, consider the next prerequisite of friendship and relational love, which is that all individuals in a relationship must possess the power to affect one another through their actions. Friendship cannot exist between two or more beings unless those beings have the ability to interact with one another and the capacity to affect each other in some manner. There are many different types of forums that could provide beings with the ability to affect one another through their actions. These forums do not even have to be physical; but, because humans are physical beings who exist in a material universe, the discussion that follows is limited to the material realm.

Imagine a universe consisting of ten different Earth-like planets, each of which has a single human being living on it. Each of these ten people is fully aware of the existence of all the others yet none of them has any ability to communicate or interact with anyone else. Would friendship be possible under these conditions? Since interaction between two or more beings is necessary for the experience of friendship, friendship would obviously not be possible in such an environment.

Instead of a universe where ten different people are living on ten different planets, imagine all ten people are placed onto one planet. Now that all ten people inhabit a common forum of existence, imagine nine of the people want to be independent of everyone else, but the remaining person is adamant about establishing some sort of bond with at least one of the others. If the nine other people all refuse to take any sort of action to establish a relationship with the one person who is seeking to interact with them, can friendship occur?

Since friendship cannot be formed without two or more parties each taking some sort of action to interact with one another, it would be impossible for a friendship to form under such circumstances. Sharing a forum of existence with other beings is a necessary precondition to provide individuals with the capacity to experience friendship and relational love, but the presence of individuals in a shared forum of existence is, in itself, insufficient to guarantee the experience of friendship and love.

Now suppose that one person attempted to forcibly compel one of the others to establish a relationship with him? What if God himself arrived on the planet and commanded one of the creatures to establish a loving relationship with him,[50] making it clear to the creature that he had no choice in the matter? Can genuine friendship occur against one party's will? Again, the answer is obvious: friendship requires each party to voluntarily enter into a relationship.

What happens if all ten people, acting on their own free will, decide they are going to establish some sort of cooperative relationship with one another? Will friendship necessarily result? For example, suppose everyone decides the best way to protect himself from the elements is to work with the others to build a communal shelter. Each person then voluntarily agrees to work with everyone else in a shared effort to build a shelter for their collective use. Furthermore, each person completely trusts the others to perform the labor they promised to do as part of the joint construction project, but the sole reason each individual agrees to this arrangement is so he can benefit individually. Is friendship experienced in this scenario?

In this example, every prerequisite of love listed above is present except the last element, selflessness. There are now: (1) ten people, (2) each with the ability to affect the others through his actions, (3) each placing faith in the others, and (4) each voluntarily agreeing to exercise his power in a manner that will benefit the others. Still, friendship is absent. The reason friendship is absent is because this is a purely contractual agreement in which each party is ultimately only concerned about his own ends. As long as selflessness is absent, friendship remains absent.

It is important to pause at this juncture to clarify what is meant by the word "selflessness." Selflessness, as the term is used here, is not meant to convey the total destruction of ego. Total selflessness is as incompatible with love as total selfishness. Just as total selfishness amounts to a megalomaniacal focus on one's own importance, total selflessness equates to total loss of ego, and therefore to the loss of one's identity. If one ceases to have a distinct identity, then the first prerequisite of love is lost (the existence of two or more persons), and love becomes impossible.

Leviticus 19:18 makes this point when it states, "love your neighbor as yourself."[51] This passage does not state that individuals are to love their neighbor more than themselves, nor does it say people are to love themselves more than their neighbors. Instead, the verse calls for equilibrium between ego and selflessness, a point also made in Galatians 5:14 and James 2:8.[52]

Once the element of selflessness, thus defined, is added to the scenario above, experiences of genuine friendship and relational love become possible. True friendships come into existence only when two or more of the individuals in the example above decide to set aside their own selfish ends long enough to start caring about the welfare of others, then act accordingly. Love becomes possible when selflessness reaches the point at which each person has as much concern about the well-being of others as he has for himself, then acts in a manner commensurate with this concern.

GOD IS ALL-JUST

To understand the basis of a concept as amorphous as "justice," it is necessary to first understand the basis of man's thinking and reasoning. While a discussion of the philosophy of reasoning may not initially appear relevant to the problem of pain, it will become clear in Part II that the analysis in this chapter does, in fact, serve an important role in answering the problem of pain. Specifically, the analysis in this chapter is necessary to understand the pivotal role of faith in man's reasoning, as well as the central role of faith in man's ability to experience love.

Philosophers have long grappled with questions about the nature and source of justice. Some argue that people's concept of justice is derived from a fluid set of social and cultural norms, which means humanity's perception of justice can differ considerably from one society to the next. Others believe man's understanding of justice is based on fixed, absolute principles that take the same basic form everywhere, which suggests there is a universal code of morality all of humanity recognizes innately.

This latter position is the basis of a juridical theory known as "natural law," the operation of which is described in the *Catechism* as follows: "Application of the natural law varies greatly; it can demand reflection that takes account of various conditions of life according to places, times, and circumstances. Nevertheless, in the diversity of cultures, the natural law remains a rule that binds men among themselves and imposes on them, beyond the inevitable differences, common principles."[53]

In the end, whether a person subscribes to the concept of natural law or to the idea that justice is derived from fluid social and cultural norms, both of these bases for justice rely on at least one assumption that cannot be proven with absolute certainty. Carefully analyze any argument that purports to explain the source of justice, and it will soon become apparent that the argument relies on at least one premise that cannot be definitively proven. Indeed, this is the case with all logical proofs, regardless of the topic of inquiry.

Take the famous example of René Descartes's attempt to construct a logical proof of the seemingly obvious proposition that man exists.[54] At first glance, this topic of inquiry may seem like the height of nonsense. The issue is important, however, because it goes to the root of whether a logic-based foundation truly exists for knowledge of any kind.

Because this inquiry is one that initially strikes most people as quite odd, it may help to think about it in this way: people rely on their minds to understand the world around them. Many do this without ever questioning whether man's mind is a reliable instrument for acquiring knowledge. Because man is stuck relying on his own mind to assess whether his thinking is sound, man has no way to be certain his thoughts are free of delusion. If no one can be fully certain that any given thought is free of delusion, how can a person be certain of his thinking when it tells him that he exists?

Descartes's answer was this: "I think, therefore I am."[55] Said another way, "I may not be able to trust in the soundness of a single thought I have, but the mere fact that I engage in the act of thinking is proof that I exist. I think, therefore I am."

On the surface, this argument appears sound. But upon further reflection, it becomes apparent that even this most basic of arguments contains a fallacy. Descartes seeks to prove that he exists as a being. But with the first word of his argument ("I") Descartes presupposes the very thing he seeks to prove ("I am"). In other words, Descartes starts by assuming his existence, and then concludes by asserting his existence. The argument "*I* think, therefore *I* am" is circular.

Descartes's argument is hardly unique in this regard. All human reasoning, without exception, begins with at least one assumed premise. Human logic cannot start from zero, without some sort of presupposed truth claim, even if that truth claim is something as ostensibly obvious as the assertion that man exists.

In order to assess the legitimacy of an argument that is based off of an assumed truth claim, some sort of independent criterion must be identified by which to judge the validity of the argument's starting presupposition. Once an independent criterion has been identified to assess the validity of an argument's starting presupposition, the soundness of this supposedly "independent" criterion must then be demonstrated.

The problem, of course, is that this independent criterion is itself an assumption, or is based on an assumption. In order to maintain the logical integrity of the argument, the validity of this second assumption must be examined as well. But to test the validity of this second assumption, an argument or an inquiry must be constructed that relies on yet another assumption. The process of questioning and testing assumptions continues on and on, into infinity. Human reasoning starts with assumption, and there is no way to get in front of the use of assumption through the application of reason.[56]

If human reasoning rests on assumption, then it is only sensible to ask what it means to "assume" something. Perhaps the most straightforward explanation is this: an assumption is something that cannot be proven with absolute logical certainty. More specifically, an assumption is some sort of concept, idea, thought, or theory a person accepts or adopts even though it cannot be definitively proven true.

When a person accepts an assumption as a truth, that assumption is called a "belief." All beliefs ultimately rest on some degree of faith. While a persuasive case can often be made for a person believing in some particular concept or idea, the nature of every belief is that it is based on faith at some level or another.

Human reasoning is based on assumption, which means human reasoning is ultimately based on faith. Because every argument begins with at least one faith-based assumption, it is fair to say that faith is the foundation of human reasoning.[57] As Paul Tillich writes in *Dynamics of Faith*, "Faith precedes all attempts to derive it from something else, because these attempts are themselves based on faith."[58]

With this background, the pivotal role that faith plays in man's thinking about "justice" can now be better understood. Since all arguments concerning the nature of justice rely on at least one presupposition that cannot be definitely proven, these arguments can never explain what is "just" or "fair" with logical certainty. If a person declares that he has identified what is "just" using a logic-based proof, it is only because he has duped himself, or is trying to dupe his audience, into believing at least one assumption that he cannot possibly prove through the use of pure reason. Since the starting point of every argument on justice is some type of assumption that must ultimately be taken on faith, the conclusions of such arguments are little more than beliefs. Starting assumptions determine what is meant when one declares, "God is perfectly just."

In Part II, orthodox Christian doctrine is used to provide key assumptions concerning God's justice. A person's acceptance of these assumptions is ultimately a matter of faith; none can be definitively proven to be true or untrue. But, as the discussion above shows, it is impossible for people to escape faith-based reasoning on issues that determine their worldview, no matter what arguments a person may ultimately find persuasive. An individual may fully believe that he is totally free of faith-based influences on matters of political, ideological, or philosophical concern to him, yet as convinced as he may be of the unassailable logic of his own thinking, his reasoning still rests on faith.

When it comes to questions about religious matters, the foundational role of faith in man's reasoning should be obvious. Whenever man focuses his mind on questions about God, he is inevitably cornered into making a fundamental faith-based judgment in favor of God or against him. Perhaps it should be expected that man's reasoning about God always leads him to a decisive point of faith-based decision-making. After all, if love between man and God is indeed the principal purpose of man's creation, and if faith is required to experience love, man's inability to avoid faith-based thinking with respect to God could very well be the result of purposeful design. Man's mind may have been deliberately structured in such a way that man has no option but to make a faith-based choice either for or against God.

Irrespective of whether this is the case, it is important to acknowledge the reality of man's cognitive state. The failure to recognize that man's reasoning relies upon faith-based assumptions leads to the arrogance of believing that certain arguments are impervious to attack. *Every* argument ultimately rests on at least one faith-based assumption, usually many. The arguments in this book are not exceptions, and for this reason, key assumptions are stated plainly.[59]

With respect to God's justice, the key faith-based presuppositions that underpin the arguments in this book are these:

(1) A perfectly just, law-giving God will not look the other way when a wrongful act is committed, pretending as though that act never transpired. Consequently, if the scales of justice are thrown into imbalance as the result of a wrongful or unjust act, something must eventually be done to put those scales back into alignment. This requires that immoral or wrongful decisions, however one defines them, ultimately be paid for or become neutralized in some manner. If they are not, perfect justice is compromised. For this reason, as stated in First John 4:10, it is assumed that some form of recompense is necessary for wrongdoing.[60]

(2) The fair and just penalty for committing an act that undermines love is that the wrongdoer's being— which, it is further assumed, was created for the express purpose of engaging in a loving relationship with God—is itself undermined, resulting in the experience of pain, suffering, and death.[61] (Man's status as a being specifically designed to engage in a timeless loving relationship with God is a multifaceted issue that is developed in detail in Part II.)

GOD IS ALL-WISE

The assertion "God is all-wise" is the last of the four divine character traits that must be briefly examined before the solution to the problem of pain can be provided. For the purposes of the arguments in this book, it is assumed that God, in his wisdom, prioritizes love before justice. It is further assumed that God, in his wisdom, prioritizes love over his own suffering, human suffering, angelic suffering, and the suffering of all creatures in the natural world.

With these assumptions in mind, imagine the following scenario: God creates two human beings, vesting each with power to affect God, one another, and lesser creatures. The two human beings can decide to use their power for the sake of benefiting others, but they are also free to use it in furtherance of a selfish objective. If they decide to use their power for the sake of benefiting one another, they will enjoy the central purpose of their existence—the experience of love with God and with one another.

However, if they decide to use their power in pursuit of a selfish end, they will undermine the very reason for their existence, with the result that they will create enormous suffering for themselves and for all creatures whom God has given them power to affect. God cannot usurp this decision-making from the first humans without undermining their ability to experience love, which means that responsibility for exercising this power must reside with them.

Since God knows in advance that humanity will often abuse the power that he has given them, God's decision to vest man with this power is one that entails known costs. If the benefits nonetheless outweigh these costs, then the decision to vest humanity with such power is a wise one. This is the key issue that must be considered when assessing the wisdom of God's decision to prioritize love before justice, as well as his decision to prioritize love over suffering.

Without delving into the various facets of this issue, the most crucial of which will be examined in Part II, it is worth briefly considering what is so unique and important about love that God would place it at the pinnacle of his value structure. Love's pre-eminence above all other ends stems from the requirement that each actor, including God himself, must willingly exercise power for the benefit of others while also voluntarily relinquishing a certain amount of control over his own being to the influence of others. Love therefore requires each individual in a relationship to engage in two distinct acts, the first of which can be characterized as the *eros* act, and the second of which can be labeled the *agape* act.

The *eros* component consists of the pursuit of self-fulfillment via the object of a person's affection, while the *agape* component consists of the willingness to self-surrender for the sake of the other being.[62] Love results from the concurrent exchange of both *eros* and *agape*—of power that is simultaneously exercised for one's own benefit and for the benefit of another being, together with surrender to that other being's concomitant exercise of power for the same purposes. It is this interplay of surrender and control, which is ultimately based on the level of faith each being has in the other, that gives love its significance, uniqueness, and im-measurable worth.

The reason faith is essential to this equation is straightfor-ward. One does not willingly expose a portion of his own being to influence or control by another person unless he has faith that the other person will act in a beneficent manner toward him. Faith is therefore essential to love.

The forms that love can take are as varied as the circumstances in which individuals are able to interact with others and affect them through their decision-making. Consequently, love can oc-cur not only within families and between neighbors in the ordi-nary settings of domestic life; love can also occur in the extreme environs of war, where soldiers are forced to place faith in one another for the sake of their very lives. Indeed, some of the most powerful friendships develop in the midst of armed conflict due to the tremendous faith soldiers must often place in each other.

These deep bonds of friendship serve as the motivation for the most heralded acts of battlefield sacrifice, the kind where a person jumps on a live grenade or rushes headlong into direct enemy fire in order to save a friend. Combat veterans who have known friendships of this magnitude frequently rank them among the finest experiences of their lives.[63] Such friendships may not have even been possible in a peacetime setting where the risk of death was not ever-present.

This phenomenon raises a singularly important question: is the experience of friendship and love really so valuable that it outweighs the experience of suffering, fear, injustice, and death?[64] As will become clear by the end of this book, the answer to the problem of pain ultimately hinges on this question.

PART II:
CREATION, FALL, AND TIMELESS BEING

The study of "last things," a theological subject called "eschatology," has long been a dominant concern of Christian thinkers. Though a considerable body of work on this topic has accumulated over the centuries, few theologians have thought to apply eschatological ideas to understand the nature of man's existence before the fall. Part II utilizes theological concepts that have emerged from the study of man's eternal fate to provide insights into the timeless nature of man's existence prior to the fall.

A little background on this area of Christian thought is helpful to lay the groundwork for the arguments that follow. Several decades ago, the esteemed theologian Joseph Ratzinger, who became Pope Benedict XVI in 2005, wrote a book titled *Eschatology: Death and Eternal Life*. In it, he discusses the concept of timeless existence in the afterlife, using phrases such as the "end of time" and "non-time" to describe it. He writes, "the end of time is itself no longer time. It is not a date which happens to come extremely late in the calendar but rather non-time."[65]

In the book, Ratzinger tries to imagine the operation of matter in the new creation that resurrected man is prophesied to inhabit. Because Ratzinger adheres to the orthodox Christian belief that man will be physically resurrected, and because he also maintains that matter in the restored creation will not be ordered around time-based rules of physics, he reasons that the "resurrection... presuppose[s] a completely different kind of matter, a fundamentally transformed cosmos."[66]

In this eternal realm—where time itself does not exist—matter will no longer be governed by the principles of "space-time" that are the mainstay of modern physics. Because matter is inextricably interwoven with time in the present universe, few if any of the discoveries that physicists have made about the operation of matter in the space-time cosmos are relevant to understanding how matter operates in a cosmos where time itself does not exist. Since man is a material being, this means that even the resurrected bodies of mankind will operate in a fundamentally different manner than they do now.

If time itself will not exist in the final state, and if the final state will be similar to that which existed at the very beginning of creation, this means that man existed in a state of "non-time" prior to the fall. But what is the practical reality of existing in a supratemporal state of being? How does physics work when it is not based on the principles of space-time?

Though it is impossible to provide much more than surface-level answers to these questions, they can still be answered with enough clarity to reconcile the account of man's direct creation in Genesis with the well-established findings of astronomy, evolutionary biology, and other fields of natural science that provide a window into the distant past. This is the focus of the opening chapter of Part II.

IN THE BEGINNING

Genesis 1 presents creation as the work of God. A sharp contrast is drawn between the purpose for which man was created and the purpose for which plants and animals were created. Whereas Genesis 1:11 describes the creation of plant life with the words, "God said, 'Let the earth put forth vegetation,'" and Genesis 1:24 describes the creation of animal life with the words, "Let the earth bring forth living creatures according to their kinds," Genesis 1:26–27 describes the creation of man with the following language: "Then God said, 'Let us make man in our image, after our likeness; and let them have dominion over the fish in the sea, and over the birds of the air, and over the cattle, and over all the earth, and over every creeping thing that creeps upon the earth.' So God created man in his own image."[67]

This language clearly communicates that man was made sovereign over the other forms of life described in Genesis 1. As such, man determines the fate of all life within this creation, as well as his own fate, through the exercise of his will.

According to the *Catechism of the Catholic Church*, in addition to being sovereign over other physical creatures, man is distinguishable from them in his ability to "know and love his creator."[68] While other physical creatures exist in dependence on one another, to complete and to complement one another "in the service of each other,"[69] man is "the only creature on earth that God has willed for its own sake."[70] He alone is called to "share, by knowledge and love, in God's own life."[71]

This latter assertion is based in significant part on the language of Genesis 1:26 and 5:1, declaring that man is the only creature on Earth made in the "likeness" of God.[72] In order to better understand the meaning of Genesis 1:26 and 5:1, one must have at least a rudimentary understanding of what God is "like." For this, it is necessary to briefly digress from the creation narrative in Genesis in order to examine the doctrine of the Trinity.

According to this doctrine, God is a unity of three distinct persons: Father, Son, and Holy Spirit.[73] Something analogous to a "society" exists between these three persons, with each one engaging in all of the reciprocities of faith and selflessness required for the experience of relational love.[74] The love between them is so perfect, so total, that it forms a single unified being—the being called "God." In other words, God's very personhood is the "product" of perfect love; God is, quite literally, the personification of love. As First John 4:8 states, "God *is* love." [Emphasis added.][75]

Man, to the extent he follows the example of the Trinity, is likewise a loving unity.[76] Made as "Male and female,"[77] the body of a man forms a unity with that of a woman to become "one flesh,"[78] in order to beget another in love. The *Catechism* states, "This partnership of man and woman constitutes the first form of communion between persons."[79] It further states that "there is a...resemblance between the unity of the divine persons and the fraternity that men are to establish among themselves in truth and love."[80]

Being made in the likeness of God, man is called to mimic the loving ways of his Creator. "God who created man out of love also calls him to love—the fundamental and innate vocation of every human being. For man is created in the image and likeness of

God who is himself love."[81] Specifically, man is called to enter into loving relationships with God and with other human beings, the former of whom man is commanded to love "with all your heart, and with all your soul, and with all your mind," and the latter of whom man is commanded to love "as yourself."[82]

As was discussed in Part I, individuals cannot experience loving relationships with one another without all five prerequisites of relational love being met. As a reminder, the prerequisites of relational love are as follows:

(1)   Two (or more) persons;

(2)   Both (or all) of whom possess the power to affect one another through their actions;

(3)   Each must voluntarily;

(4)   Place faith in one another to treat each other in a beneficent manner; and

(5)   Act selflessly toward one another.

Returning to Genesis, this means the first humans must have existed as independent beings who were capable of affecting both God and each other through their actions. In addition, they must have been capable of placing faith in one another. Furthermore, the first humans must have been imbued with at least some form of free will, and this free will must have included the capacity to engage in at least one egocentric act.

According to Genesis 2:16–17, the selfish act left open to them was a choice to care more about the acquisition of a form of knowledge than to care about their relationship with God or their mate.[83] This choice, or one like it, was necessary to give them the opportunity to experience relational love. After all, in order for a reciprocal loving relationship to be experienced, each individual in the relationship must be willing to eschew the pursuit of self-serving ends that can only be acquired at the expense of the others. Decision-making of this kind cannot occur in the absence of a *genuine* opportunity to choose between selflessness and self-centeredness.

The account of man's life in Eden that is provided in Genesis 2 indicates that the first humans enjoyed the experience of love with God and with one another as long as everyone continued to make the voluntary decision to care as much about the others as they cared about themselves.[84] But, if man decided to exercise his free will to place a selfish interest over his relationship with God, the entire reason for his existence would be undermined, with the result that his life would cease. This outcome of selfishness was stated unequivocally by God the Father in Genesis 2:16–17 when he cautioned Adam, "You may freely eat of every tree of the garden; but of the tree of the knowledge of good and evil you shall not eat, for in the day that you eat of it you shall die."[85]

Genesis 3 asserts that the first humans decided to exercise their free will to place a selfish interest over their relationship with God when they availed themselves of their power to pursue the one selfish end that was left open to them. The reward, or fruit, of this decision was the acquisition of a form of knowledge that had hitherto been absent from their minds: knowledge of good and evil. Specifically, man had acquired knowledge of good through his newfound awareness of the different material and experiential forms of good in his environment, and man had acquired knowledge of evil through his newfound awareness of the different self-centered actions he could take in order to obtain or enjoy all of this good by prioritizing his acquisition of it over love.

"Evil" can therefore be defined as any willful choice to pursue an objective that can only be acquired or experienced at the expense of love.[86] This definition means:

(1) Knowledge of evil is distinct from evil itself. Evil itself requires a *choice*, not simply an awareness of a choice.

(2) God is not the creator of evil if he never exercises his will to pursue an objective that can only be acquired at the expense of love. Therefore, if God created beings with free will for the sake of allowing them to experience love, God is not the creator of evil if these beings later decide to exercise their free will in a manner that undermines love.[87]

(3) A creature who does not have knowledge of good and evil can nonetheless commit evil if that creature makes a willful choice to pursue an objective that undermines love. One cannot make a willful choice to undermine love unless one first understands what love is. Because the first humans understood what love is through personal experience, they were aware that it was wrong to reject love in favor of another end. As a result, the first humans can rightly be held accountable for their initial act of sin even though they did not have knowledge of good and evil when they committed this act.

It is important to note that the act of original sin required Adam and Eve to abandon their faith in God. This is made apparent by the fact that God specifically warned them that if they ate of the tree of knowledge of good and evil, they would die. For Adam and Eve to have nonetheless eaten can only mean that they chose to believe that God was lying. There can be no clearer abandonment of faith than this.[88] Because faith is an essential prerequisite of relational love, faithlessness is a core feature of all sin.[89]

One of the consequences of man's original sin was a change in his underlying nature. Prior to his adoption of evil, man was predisposed toward selflessness. When man decided to prioritize the acquisition of a selfish objective over his relationship with God, greed replaced selflessness as the predominant force governing his thinking, desires, and behavior. This change not only undermined man's ability to experience wholly loving relationships with others, it also made him susceptible to pain, suffering, and death.[90] Simply put, man had become a "fallen" being.

It is essential to understand the description of man's fall in Genesis 3 as an account of an actual event, not a fictitious tale meant merely to impart a lesson about sin. The Catholic Church's teaching on this point is unambiguous and consistent: "The account of the fall in *Genesis* 3 uses figurative language, but affirms a primeval event, a deed that took place *at the beginning of the history of man.*"[91]

In spite of the Church's insistence that Genesis 3 describes a real incident, some believers are nonetheless inclined to regard the account of man's fall as a mere metaphorical story with no basis in fact. This mistake is often due to readers' propensity to impose their own lived experience of linear time and finite being onto the account of man's existence prior to the fall, rather than seeking to understand Genesis 1–3 in the context of the first humans' experience of timeless being.

By way of introduction to this topic, it must be recognized that, because the first humans were not susceptible to death prior to their commission of sin, they would have had no endpoint by which to measure their existence. Consequently, they would not have experienced any sense of temporality whatsoever. On this point alone, it should be evident that mankind's present experience of time and being is considerably different than the state of existence initially experienced by the first humans. This is by no means the only difference, however.

In order to more fully appreciate how monumentally at odds mankind's current experience of time and being is from the state of existence experienced by the first humans, careful consideration must be given to what an uncompromised loving relationship with God would be like. For this, one must try to imagine a state of relational being that stands outside of the construct of time. This state of being exists beyond time because the relationship under consideration is one between man, at a period when his life was experienced in a timeless state of existence not subject to death, and the eternal,[92] omnibenevolent God, who supersedes all categories of finite existence.

The assertion that God supersedes all categories of finite existence means God exists before time, within time, after time, and beyond time;[93] he is not constrained in any manner by space or distance; he exceeds all limits of materialism and physicality. This understanding of God is affirmed in the *Catechism*, which states that God is "not limited by space and time but able to be present how and when he wills;"[94] he exists "beyond time and space."[95] To grasp what an uncompromised loving relationship with such a being is like, one must therefore attempt to think beyond every category of physical and time-based limitation through which and within which mankind currently experiences life. Only then can the first humans' experience of communion with God in a state of transcendent, timeless being be understood in its proper context.

A degree of insight into the nature of this state of existence is provided through various biblical passages describing redeemed man's experience of communion with God. In reference to this state of being, First Corinthians 13:8 describes the passing away of "knowledge" and other temporal-based matters, which are replaced by an experience of timeless love with God.[96] Matthew 24:35 likewise describes how the Earth and heavenly bodies that exist today will "pass away," suggesting that what follows will take place in a wholly different state of being than the one man now experiences.[97]

Ephesians 3:19 describes this state of being as an experience of "love…which surpasses knowledge" and as the experience of being "filled with all the fullness of God."[98] Philippians 4:7 describes the "peace of God" that is experienced in this state of being as one "which passes all understanding."[99] First Corinthians 15:28 describes a state of existence in which God becomes "all in all" as his love fills up and envelops all those in communion with him.[100]

These descriptions of the eternal state give some sense of the state of being that the first humans may have experienced prior to the fall. Of course, without experiencing such a state of being, it is impossible to truly understand what it entails. The Old Testament suggests this state of being is in fact so radically different than the one that fallen humanity experiences that anyone wishing to completely understand it would be required to suffer the death of his own temporal existence. This is indicated in Exodus 33:19–20 when, in response to Moses's request to be shown the "glory" of God, Moses is told: "'I will make all my goodness pass before you, and will proclaim before you my name… But,' he said, 'you cannot see my face; for man shall not see me and live.'"[101]

Even though Moses's interactions with God were constrained in this manner, these interactions were nonetheless so powerful that they caused the skin of Moses's face to shine with a radiance that caused his followers to be "afraid to come near him."[102] If even such circumscribed interactions with God affect man in this manner, one can scarcely fathom what an uncompromised loving relationship in the direct presence of God would be like. This is what the first humans experienced.

Genesis 3 states that this relationship with God was ruptured through a choice that was freely made by the first humans, wherein they prioritized the acquisition of a lesser end over their loving relationship with God. This choice represents a dramatic inflection point in man's experience of time and being because Genesis 3 is describing nothing less than the termination of a state of being in which man exists in a timeless loving relationship with God himself.

Given the nature of the relationship that the first humans experienced with God at the outset of their existence, it should come as no surprise that the rupture of this relationship would produce consequences that affect every aspect of their progeny's existence. There is no reason to believe that any aspect of the created order that was made subject to man's dominion was able to escape massive disruption, reversal, and upending. Indeed, because the relationship that was ruptured was one that occurred in a supratemporal state of being, the implications of this rupture can likewise be expected to supersede time, changing the order and basis of everything within the domain God had given to man, at all points in existence.

This is what makes the fall such an extraordinary event. Its scope is massive to the point of being nearly incomprehensible to finite beings who experience existence locked within the one-directional flow of linear time because it involves the rupture of an intimate relationship with an omnipotent being who exceeds in infinite measure every linear, spatial, and materialistic category through which mankind now understands his existence. The account of the fall is, for this reason, an account of an utterly radical transformation in man's experience of time, being, and place.

The fall also represents a radical transformation of all creatures placed under mankind's dominion because this realm of life, like man himself prior to the fall, existed in a state of being that superseded the limitations of time, space, and physicality as humanity currently understands and experiences them. The transformation of this domain into a fallen state of existence entailed all life under man's authority changing from an existence of loving cooperation with all other creatures[103] into a wholly new state of existence that aligns with man's new self-centered nature. When man oriented himself toward selfishness at the time of the fall, all that God had placed under man's sovereign dominion likewise fell into selfishness. Man's entire domain became a self-serving free-for-all, which meant a vicious, violent, and deadly existence for all life.

It is imperative to understand that this transformation occurs at *all* points in the history of existence and in *every* corner of the physical dimension over which man was given dominion, because man and everything placed under his authority transformed from what was once a selfless, transcendent state of being—superseding time—into a selfish state of being that is finite and linear, where physical death can occur. This can be a challenging concept to grasp, but it must be recognized that the transformation of timeless, godlike beings to temporal existence, resulting from a freely chosen transformation to self-centeredness, includes the imprinting of this self-centeredness across the entirety of their domain.

Said another way, when man's domain changed from a timeless state of existence to a time-based one as the result of man's willful adoption of selfishness, man's newly acquired self-centeredness was imposed on all aspects of his domain, everywhere and all at once. As Joseph Ratzinger writes, "non-time, ...since it is outside of time, is equally close to every time."[104] Consequently, every aspect of both man and the creatures placed under his dominion underwent a wholesale fall into self-centered existence, a state of existence that is imposed throughout the entire temporal sphere, from the inception of linear time to the end of linear time. This has critically important implications for understanding the foundation of the temporal history of life on Earth.

The scientific theory of evolution by natural selection has been thought by many to contradict Genesis 1–3, but a proper understanding of the fall shows that the reverse is actually true. The indifferent, individualist mechanisms that underlie evolution fully comport with the account of the fall in Genesis because the driving forces that propel evolution are in perfect accord with the uncaring, self-centered motivations that man decided to act upon when he turned his back on God.

Since man is the sovereign ruler of all creatures within his domain, every element of these creatures' existence mirrors the will of man when he existed as a timeless being, at all points in linear time. When the will of man in a timeless state of existence became individualistic in its focus, and indifferent in its concern about other beings, every aspect of man's domain emulated this change, at all points across the full continuum of existence. Evolution, then, is evidence of a foundational reordering of man's realm of existence, resulting from the first humans' decision-making when they existed in a supratemporal state of being.

Change of this size and scope may seem far beyond the powers and influence of man, but this is not what is asserted in Genesis. When Genesis 1:26 declares that man was made in God's "likeness" for the purpose of enabling them to exercise "dominion over" all the creatures in the realm given to them by God, it should be apparent that these two assertions are not meant to imply a form of dominion like that exercised by a zookeeper over the animals in his charge. The "dominion" referenced in Genesis 1:26 is instead one of divine scope and scale; it is a form of rule that includes the godlike power to reorder the very basis of all life placed under man's sovereignty.

The notion that God created man with a nature and stature like God's own finds ample support in the New Testament, most crucially in the person of Jesus Christ. Throughout his public ministry Jesus repeatedly referred to himself as the "Son of man," an unmistakable reference to his human lineage. Jesus also stated that he is the Son of God the Father, a point he made unequivocally during his trial before the Sanhedrin, described in Mark 14:61–62 as follows: "Again the high priest asked him, 'Are you the Christ, the Son of the Blessed?' 'I am,' said Jesus, 'And you will see the Son of man sitting at the right hand of Power and coming with the clouds of heaven.'"[105]

Christ is the fusion of God and man in one person, fully God and fully man.[106] Two beings with fundamentally different essences cannot produce offspring together without that offspring being a corruption of the essences of both parents. Just as a reptile and a human cannot beget offspring without that offspring being a corruption of the essences of both of its parents, God the Father cannot beget offspring with a being that is fundamentally different from him without that offspring being a corruption of God's essence.

This means that if man had not been created as a being with *truly* divine-like stature, God and man could not exist as a unity in the person of Jesus Christ, a perfect being in whom God the Father declares he is "well pleased."[107] God the Father would not declare that he is "well pleased" with his "only-begotten Son"[108] if Jesus were a corruption of the Father's essence. Further evidence of Christ's similitude with God the Father appears in John 14:9, when Jesus declares: "He who has seen me has seen the Father."[109] These and similar assertions have numerous important implications, one of which is this: if Jesus is the begotten Son of both God the Father and man, then the very nature of Christ's composition as a being serves as evidence of the divine-like stature of man.

First Corinthians 6:3 provides further support for the assertion that man in an unfallen state is vested with divine-like stature and authority. In reference to man's power and influence in the eternal state, the Apostle Paul writes, "Do you not know that we are to judge angels?"[110] Man would only be in a position to judge angels if man became unified with God himself.

One of the core tenets of the Catholic Church is that man's divinization is the ultimate purpose of mankind's creation.[111] This concept is expressed in various New Testament passages, including Second Peter 1:4, which states that redeemed man is to "become partakers of the divine nature" through Christ.[112] Paul describes this unification to the very being of God in First Corinthians 12, writing that redeemed man will become "one body" with God.[113] The *Catechism* declares, "The ultimate end of the whole divine economy is the entry of God's creatures into the perfect unity of the Blessed Trinity."[114] In *Timaeus*, Plato provides the reason God chose this creative goal: "Let me tell you then why the creator made this world of generation. He was good, and the good can never have any jealousy of anything. And being free from jealousy, he desired that all things should be as like himself as they could be."[115]

If it is true that man was made with a nature and stature that would allow him to become a unity with God, then there is nothing unreasonable about the idea that man in a timeless unfallen state would possess the godlike power to change the underlying nature of the creatures placed under his authority, at all points across the entire continuum of these creatures' existence. Certainly, God could do this through a single act of his will. If so, logic dictates that timeless beings who have been made in the "likeness" of God can do the same.

The immensity of the first humans' power over both their own nature and the creatures placed under their dominion is a measure of the immensity of the fall. It must be remembered that Genesis is a book about divine matters, not mere terrestrial concerns. For this reason, the account of man's existence in Eden must not be read as if it were describing two individuals' lives in a temporal, earthly garden plot. To approach it in such a manner is to suffer from a poverty of critical thinking that limits reality to only that which can be seen through the myopic lens of finite, earthly existence.[116]

The failure to think in infinite, divine paradigms has led many to blindly insist that the central tenets of Christianity contradict the geologic record and other scientifically verifiable aspects of reality, when in fact Christianity points to a vastly greater reality. That reality is this: God created man with divine-like stature and power for the purpose of enabling man to *fully* share God's life and being in a timeless love-based union.[117]

The first humans' stature and power were in fact so much like God's that, through the exercise of their will, they reordered even the basis of the material realm itself. This point is clearly made in Genesis 3:17 when, following Adam's original sin, God said to him, "cursed is the ground because of you."[118] The "ground" refers to the matter out of which the world is made. It consists of the chemical elements listed in the periodic table, and it adheres to the same laws of physics that govern the operation of matter everywhere in the universe. The fact that the universe contains an enormous amount of "ground" in it does not conflict with the assertion that unfallen man, who was made in the "likeness" of almighty God, possessed the capacity to alter the manner in which all of this material operates.[119]

A similar analysis applies when considering the age of the universe. That the universe is billions of years old is in no way incompatible with the assertion that Adam and Eve, who were timeless beings made in the likeness of the eternal God, had the capacity to determine the trajectory of the fallen universe's entire temporal history, from beginning to end.[120] Again, it is essential to recognize that time is altogether inferior to godlike beings who exist in a supratemporal state, for they are ever-present beings. It follows that the will of Adam and Eve would be reflected in every aspect of their realm, at all points in existence.

Fallen man's warped obsession with materialism, together with his undue fixation on time, has a way of clouding his reasoning. The colossal size and age of the universe in no way means that it is impervious to systemic change by beings made in the "likeness" of the omnipotent, eternal God. Given the nature of timeless being, and the vast power possessed by beings who exercise "dominion" in a manner genuinely like that of God,[121] it is a misconception to think that Adam and Eve did not have the ability to change the very foundation of the material realm itself.

Fallen man's preoccupation with materialism and time is also the source of his tendency to conflate matter and age with value. The Bible teaches that this is a grievous error, a point made by the short, materially impoverished, yet invaluable life of Jesus Christ. Because of man's excessive regard for materialism and age, when man stares out at the universe, he has a tendency to think of himself as a triviality in comparison to the immensity and age of that which he sees. In so doing, man engages in the fallacy of thinking his importance can somehow be measured by comparing his physical stature and longevity as a fallen being against the size and age of the universe. But this is to assign value on the bases of mass, space, and time, which is plainly absurd. Mass, space, and time are matters that belong to the realm of physics. Value, in contrast, is a concept that belongs to the moral sphere.

The Bible is a book about man's moral life, and it stresses that man's moral decision-making has divine consequences. The statement in Genesis 3:17 that the "ground" became "cursed" because of the immoral decision-making of Adam and Eve is an unambiguous assertion that man's moral decisions are of such enormous importance that the physical order itself—that is, physics, which encompasses matter, space, and time—is subject to it. In other words, man's godlike power is employed to its greatest effect through the exercise of man's moral will.

In the darkness of man's present state of sinful being, man struggles to envision how he could possibly exercise command over the material order itself, which appears to operate in accordance with incontrovertible laws of physics. But in a sinless state of existence, man's control over the material order is patently clear. This point is made not only in Genesis 3:17, but also in various New Testament passages in which Christ displays the power of sinless man over the material realm through the performance of physical miracles.

John 2:1–11, for instance, recounts an event in which Jesus turns water into wine.[122] Luke 8:22–25 tells of an incident in which Jesus silences a raging storm at sea, causing the wind to cease blowing and the waves to calm.[123] Matthew 14:13–21 and Luke 9:10–17 describe an episode when Jesus multiplies five loaves of bread and two fish into a quantity sufficient to feed thousands of people.[124] Matthew 14:22–33 describes an event in which Jesus walks on water. In this particular event, Jesus makes it apparent that it is not only he who has the power to exercise command over the material order, but others as well: "And Peter answered him, 'Lord, if it is you, bid me come to you on the water.' He said, 'Come.' So Peter got out of the boat and walked on the water and came to Jesus."[125]

In Matthew 17:20, Jesus makes it abundantly clear that God created mankind with dominion over the physical realm itself: "I say to you, if you have faith the size of a mustard seed, you will say to this mountain, 'Move from here to there,' and it will move. Nothing will be impossible for you."[126] Because matter will be subordinate to redeemed man when he becomes one with God in the eternal state, man engages in completely backward thinking when he looks out at the vastness and age of the material realm and then regards himself as a triviality. If man is awed by the enormity and ancientness of the universe, he should be even more awed by the immensity of the stature God has given him as a being because the Bible clearly instructs that man was created with power over the very foundation of the physical realm he inhabits.

The Bible further instructs that man was made with power to reorder his own creation, down to the most elemental aspects of his own being. According to Genesis 2:7, man was formed "of dust from the ground."[127] Genesis 3:17 declares that man altered the operation of this same "ground" through his decision-making.[128] Together, these two verses communicate that man's power in his original state was so prodigious that he was able to change the structural basis of his own being, a truly godlike act because it constituted a literal reordering of his own creation.

With this reordering of his own creation because of sin, Genesis 2:16–17 asserts that man became subject to death.[129] Eternal beings cannot die, for the simple reason that there is no endpoint to eternity. This means that Adam and Eve must have undergone a change from a transcendent, timeless state of existence to a finite, temporal one. A finite, temporal existence requires the advent of time itself. Such an existence requires, in other words, that the "timeless" pre-fallen creation transform into a time-based or "space-time" creation. *Time itself is therefore a product of original sin.*

The fall from a timeless state of existence to a time-based state of existence necessitated, furthermore, that Adam and Eve enter into temporality at some specific point in the history of linear time. Because supratemporal beings exist entirely outside of time, the first humans' point of entry into time-based existence would not need to occur at the outset of linear time. On the contrary, if the first humans' reordering of their own creation and realm of sovereignty followed the same basic sequence established by God when he created the material realm and all of the creatures that inhabit it, then man's arrival into temporal existence would occur near the end of linear history; it would constitute the final key development in a realm now ordered at every level, and at every physical and historical point in space-time, around the twin pillars of selfishness and indifference to others.

Man's late-stage arrival into temporal existence is, of course, precisely what astronomers, geologists, and biologists have discovered through their study of the history of the cosmos, the geologic history of Earth, and the history of biological life on Earth. The events revealed by scientific discoveries in these fields therefore align with the narrative in Genesis. But science is and always will be incapable of providing an answer to the principal cause of these events. Science, after all, can only study that which is already in existence; it can provide no meaningful insight into the ultimate cause of physical existence itself.[130] Genesis 1–3 provides a description of the original cause of everything in physical existence, but the description it provides only comports with the findings of natural science when it is recognized that Genesis 1–3 is recounting events that occurred in a supratemporal environment.

Nothing about this interpretation of Genesis 1–3 is inconsistent with the plain meaning of key words in the text, such as the word "likeness" in Genesis 1:26. Moreover, nothing about this interpretation of Genesis 1–3 is inconsistent with other parts of the Bible. Indeed, because God "inhabits eternity," according to Isaiah 57:15,[131] and because the events described in Genesis 1–3 take place in an environment where God is directly present, logic dictates that these events should be interpreted as having taken place in a supratemporal setting, as opposed to a time-based environment like the one fallen man now inhabits. Wisdom 2:23 confirms this when it states, "God created man…in the image of his own eternity."[132]

In summary, Genesis 1–3 can only be understood in its proper context when it is recognized that the modes of existence experienced by man at the outset of his existence are categorically different from those experienced by man in his present, fallen state. With this understanding, the reasonableness of reading Genesis 1–3 as a figurative description of real events should be evident. It describes the sequence of events in which God made the physical realm, then gave "dominion over" every aspect of this realm and its creaturely inhabitants to Adam and Eve, whom he made last, in his own "likeness."

Through the misuse of their godlike power, which they exercised through their moral decision-making, Adam and Eve caused all of physical creation to become a mirror of their own self-centeredness and indifference toward God. This had the effect of pulling man and everything placed under his dominion out of a timeless, transcendent existence—shared in the direct presence of the timeless, transcendent God—into a finite, time-based existence where suffering and death occur.

This change altered the foundation of the material realm, which had been placed under man's dominion, as well as life of every level of complexity, during every phase of existence. The fall, therefore, did not merely consist of the fall of man within creation; it also consisted of the fall of the created material order itself ("the ground"), as well as all creatures that inhabit this material order, at *every* point in their existence. Adam and Eve literally reset and reordered every last aspect of man's entire existence and realm of authority, at all points across the full continuum of physical creation, through the wrongful exercise of their godlike power when they "inhabited eternity" alongside God.[133]

LOVE BEFORE JUSTICE

Justice dictates that wrongful acts be punished in a manner proportionate to their severity. "Sin" is a wrongful act, synonymous with "evil."[134] Every sinful or evil act—no matter how small or insignificant it may appear to fallen mankind—is a choice that sacrifices love in exchange for some kind of reward or fruit that a self-seeking individual hopes to acquire or experience. If love is the whole purpose of creation, this means that even the most seemingly trivial sinful act undermines the entire purpose of creation.

According to Genesis 2:17 and Romans 6:23, death is the rightful and just punishment for an act of such divine import. For the reasons outlined in the chapter titled "God Is All-Just" in Part I, it is impossible to prove that death is in fact a commensurate punishment for sin. Certainly, a strong case can be made that a being who undermines the whole purpose of creation deserves to suffer death. Ultimately, however, a person either accepts or rejects this biblical assertion on the basis of faith.

In Part I, God was described as a being who is perfectly loving, perfectly just, and perfectly wise. Creation was described as a forum made for the purpose of allowing beings to experience love with one another. The prerequisites of love described in Part I include a requirement that each person in a loving relationship exercise his free will in a selfless manner. The first chapter of Part II describes the event in which the first humans, when they existed in a supratemporal state of being, ceased exercising their free will in a selfless manner. The assumptions and arguments in these chapters, together with the assumption that death is the appropriate punishment for sin, form the foundation for the arguments that follow.

When Adam and Eve decided to prioritize a selfish objective over love, they suffered spiritual death. Spiritual death consists of separation from the presence of God,[135] who is the Source of life according to Psalm 36:9. Now spiritually dead but physically alive in a fallen state, the first humans' ultimate fate depended on how God would respond to their sin. On the one hand, God could immediately impose physical death on Adam and Eve for their act of undermining love. This choice would satisfy the remaining requirements of absolute justice, but it would simultaneously defeat the entire purpose of creation. Alternatively, God could prioritize love ahead of the final imposition of divine justice, with the goal of offering redemption to fallen man.

In the last chapter of Part I, it was asserted that God, in his wisdom, places love before justice. This in no way means that God will allow justice to go unserved indefinitely. It simply means that, given a choice between prioritizing one in front of the other, God will place love before justice. In practical and historical terms, this meant that God permitted the first humans to continue to exist following their original sin, but in a fallen state, separated and isolated from God. As described in the *Catechism*: "The harmony in which [the first humans] had found themselves, thanks to original justice, is now destroyed: the control of the soul's spiritual faculties over the body is shattered; the union of man and woman becomes subject to tensions, their relations henceforth marked by lust and domination. Harmony with creation is broken: visible creation has become alien and hostile to man."[136]

This change to man raises a question that lies at the heart of the problem of pain: knowing that the first humans would commit sin, and possessing foreknowledge of the immense pain and suffering that would result from man's change to self-centeredness due to original sin, why did God not take some sort of action to prevent the negative consequences of original sin from affecting anyone other than the first humans? For example, if God had simply devised a way to shelter other beings from the negative consequences of the sinful decision-making of the first humans, God could have prevented untold experiences of suffering.

But if God had divested human beings of their ability to affect others through their decision-making, God would have simultaneously divested humanity of its ability to experience love. The same outcome would occur if God were to divest man of any of the other prerequisites necessary for love. Once man, as a result of his sin, fell to a state of being that is susceptible to the experience of suffering and death, God could not abolish man's experience of these ills unless God:

(1) Compromised his own absolute justice by not allowing the first humans to suffer the just consequences of their wrongful decision-making;

(2) Destroyed man through the immediate imposition of both spiritual and physical death;

(3) Took away or otherwise restricted man's free will for the sake of preventing man from acting in a selfish manner; or

(4) Removed or limited man's power to affect other beings through his decision-making.

Since the first of these four actions would compromise a fundamental aspect of God's nature, God will not allow sin to go unpunished with its rightful penalty. Each of the remaining actions would destroy or undermine an essential precondition for humanity to experience love. As a result, God cannot take any of these actions without simultaneously either erasing or in some manner undermining man's ability to experience love.

Because the entire purpose of creating man is to allow man and God to experience love with one another, God judged that it is better to preserve mankind's ability to experience love than it is to spare others from the suffering that will result from man's misuse of his power. Consequently, God did not remove or diminish any powers that enabled the first humans to affect others through the exercise of their free will. But this raises another question: why did God not at least diminish man's power to the extent necessary to avoid the worst forms of suffering that man's misrule would cause others?

To the same degree that God strips man of power, God strips man of capacity to know and experience love. This applies to man's power over the creatures placed under his sovereignty, as well as to his power to create life through an act of love. Whenever such a power is taken away, there is a commensurate erosion of the scope and range of man's ability to experience love in ways that mimic God's experience of love. If God diminishes man's ability to experience any form of love, man's similarity and likeness to God is compromised. If man lacks the capacity to love at the same range and degree as God, God would have to reduce the greatness of his own being in order to join to man in an eternal loving union.

This concept can be better understood by more closely examining man's power to create life through an act of love. If man is divested of his ability to create life, then man is also denied the ability to experience the unique form of love that can only occur between a parent and child. Christ's role in the Trinity represents the inclusion of this form of love in the very makeup of God's being. Because the purpose of man's creation is to enter into an eternal loving union with God, God will not divest man of the ability to experience love that can only be enjoyed between a parent and child.[137] For God to do so would be to deny himself the experience of such love.

Of course, if God allows fallen humanity to retain the ability to create new life through an act of love, this decision will not only allow for the expansion of experiences of love; it will also lead to an expansion of experiences of suffering and death because, according to Romans 5:12, fallen man passes on his sinful nature to those whom he creates.[138] A judgment must therefore be made by God: is it more important to allow mankind the opportunity to experience the various forms of love that will occur if they are allowed to procreate, or is it more important to prevent the pain, suffering, and death that will result from fallen mankind's frequent misuse of this power?

If God, in his wisdom, ranks love over all other priorities, then the choice is clear. But, as the next chapter explains, a choice to allow man to retain the ability to create life is a choice that will require man to share in a far deeper and more difficult "likeness" of God than that which has been discussed thus far.

AN IMITATION
OF CHRIST

The suffering of innocents is one of the most difficult challenges presented by the problem of pain. This challenge can be seen starkly in the passion and crucifixion of Jesus Christ, a horrifically brutal death imposed by fallen humanity on a person entirely unblemished by sin.[139] The shocking unfairness of the suffering of innocents can likewise be witnessed in the undeserved travails of a newborn infant languishing from a debilitating illness or deformity.

Newly created life is intrinsically blameless; it has done nothing to warrant being born into a world where it will experience pain and death. Even though every person enters into existence innocent of crime or misdeed, suffering and death are the ultimate fate of all. No one, regardless of the circumstances of his birth, is spared from undeserved pain.

If God really is perfectly just and all-powerful, why does he permit all who are born into this world to be subjected to undeserved suffering? Why, moreover, does God allow even the most blameless to become victims of some of the most wretched diseases and some of the worst acts of criminality and violence?

To understand why God allows such suffering it is necessary to delve deeper into the meaning of the passages in Genesis that declare that God created humanity in his own "likeness."[140] The first chapter of Part II described how humanity shares in the likeness of God through mankind's ability to experience love, as well as through man's exercise of "dominion" over other creatures. The second chapter of Part II briefly described how humanity shares in the likeness of God through mankind's ability to create life through an act of love, but it did not fully explore the implications of this power.

Each time man creates new life, the possibility of love comes into existence where it was once absent. Each act of creating a new, free-willed human being is therefore an act that has the potential to increase the amount of love in existence. Humanity's ability to bring new life into being is, for this reason, an ability which enables mankind to serve as a partner with God in the act of fulfilling the central purpose of creation.[141]

The *Catechism* describes this partnership with God with the following language: "Called to give life, spouses share in the creative power and fatherhood of God. Married couples...are thereby cooperating with the love of God the Creator and are, in a certain sense, its interpreters."[142] The *Catechism* further states, "God thus enables men to be intelligent and free causes in order to complete the work of creation, to perfect its harmony for their own good and that of their neighbors."[143] It continues, "For it is here [in man's present state of existence] that the body of a new human family grows, foreshadowing in some way the age which is to come."[144]

But if man is to serve as a true partner with God in the enterprise of expanding the amount of love in existence, far more is required of man than merely creating new life. As was noted in the discussion of the prerequisites of love in Part I, love does not automatically occur simply because two or more independent, free-willed beings inhabit the same forum of existence. In order for love to be experienced, a certain level of sacrifice is required from each party in the relationship.

As was explained in the chapter on God's omnipotence, God's creation of new life required him to sacrifice the full exercise of his own absolute power. Specifically, God's sacrifice involved the transfer of a portion of his absolute power to his creatures in order to provide them with the ability to act independently and the capacity to experience love. Similarly, in order for love to be able to exist between human parents and their children, a certain level of sacrifice and self-renunciation is required when a man and a woman decide to bring new life of their own into the world.

For the parents, this sacrifice usually takes the form of shunning certain personal ambitions and desires to ensure that their children's needs are met. In a reflection of God's sacrifice of power when he created man, the parents of a new child must cease exercising the full scope of their power exclusively for themselves, and instead, devote a considerable portion of it to their child.

It must not be forgotten, however, that to experience love, *all* parties in a relationship must sacrifice for the benefit of one another. This means the child must also sacrifice for his parents. The form of the child's sacrifice is considerably different from that of his parents, but it still imitates a divine precedent. The sacrifice the child makes is to share in bearing the penalty of sin, even though the child did absolutely nothing to warrant this penalty.[145]

Man's experience of this undeserved suffering is essential to enabling humanity to exist as a true likeness of the Trinitarian God because, by being born into a fallen world where each child suffers for the sins of others, each person imitates Christ's suffering for love.[146] As First Peter 2:21 declares, "For to this you have been called, because Christ also suffered for you, leaving you an example, that you should follow in his steps."[147]

Hence, it is not only parents who are sacrificing as they lovingly seek to provide for their children; it is also children who are sacrificing as they endure the penalty for sin even though they, like Christ, are undeserving of this penalty. In sum, the munificent giving of the Father and the sacrificial suffering of the Son are experiences shared by both God and humanity as they partner to bring more and more love into existence through man's creation and rearing of new human life, and God's redemptive work in the fallen realm of man.

Yet, as important as it is for man to authentically share in the likeness of God through his emulation of Christ's suffering, and as important as it is for man to expand the realm of love through his creation of new life, these rationales still do not fully address the theological problems raised by the suffering of innocents. For even if man's suffering exists for the worthiest of causes, it remains the case that every newborn is subjected to unjust suffering. How can the existence of this massive injustice be reconciled with the assertion that God is perfectly just?

The answer is provided in Genesis. Man, through his original sin, and through his subsequent utilization of his power to create life, is the author of the unjust suffering of innocents. As explained in the first chapter of Part II, man's original sin changed the basis of all life placed under man's sovereign domain, which is the underlying cause of all suffering in the natural world. *Man, not God, is therefore the cause of all unjust suffering that occurs in the natural world.* Man, through the exercise of his power to create life in a sinful state of existence, is also responsible for subjecting innocent new human life to undeserved suffering.

Because God did not commit original sin on behalf of man, and because God does not exercise the power to create life on behalf of either man or the creatures within man's realm of sovereign dominion, God is not the causal agent responsible for subjecting innocent new life to unjust suffering.[148] This statement applies even to God the Father's role in introducing his only begotten Son into the fallen world of man. God the Father does not impose suffering and death on Jesus; rather, Christ voluntarily allows himself to be subjected to suffering and death at the hands of sinful man. This is made clear in John 10:18, when Jesus states, "No one takes [my life] from me, but I lay it down of my own accord. I have power to lay it down, and I have power to take it up again."[149]

Even though God never commits an unjust act by causing an innocent being to suffer, God nonetheless possesses full knowledge of the suffering and death that will result from his decision not to divest sinful mankind of its power to create life. Not a single, solitary experience of pain or suffering was unknown to God in advance of his decision to allow sinful humanity to retain its power to create life. Still, in God's judgment, the benefits of love outweigh these costs.

Some may disagree with the wisdom of God's judgment in this respect,[150] but it should be recognized that mankind makes the same basic judgment each time a man and a woman decide to exercise their power to create life. When a man and a woman make a deliberate decision to create life, they do so with the knowledge that their child will be subjected to immense undeserved suffering and will ultimately die. In spite of this, most people still decide to create life because they judge that life and love are worth these costs. If man did not make the same basic judgment as God on this matter, humanity would cease to exist.

For the first humans, the immediate consequences of this judgment are twofold. Their decision to create life enables them to experience the unique form of love that can only occur between parents and their children, but it also means that a child is brought into existence with a sinful nature. As a result of inheriting this nature from his parents, the child has no hesitancy about committing sin himself.

The existence of this new sinful being confronts God with the same choice he faced when mankind committed its very first sinful act. That choice, once more, is this: is it more important to shield others from the pain that this creature will inflict on them through his often-sinful decision-making, or is it more important that this creature be afforded the chance to experience love, to learn the preeminent value of love through his experience of it, and to have the opportunity to be redeemed?

Because the experience of love is the central purpose of creation, each generation is afforded the opportunity to experience love, with the cost that sin and its penalty are passed to each succeeding generation. The penalty for sin cannot be avoided without God either compromising his perfectly just nature by not punishing sin, or taking some sort of action to dispossess mankind of the powers that are necessary to experience love at the same range and degree as God himself does. When these powers are left in the hands of sinful mankind, love remains possible, but sin and its rightful punishment are also perpetuated.[151]

SALVATION AND
SEPARATION

I n order for the rightful penalty for sin to be overcome, someone must endure the cost of redeeming sinful mankind from the permanence of death. Why is this necessary? The reason is simple, but it requires an understanding of the workings of divine justice. In contrast to man's finite conceptions of justice, divine justice operates in modes and forms that are eternal and absolute. As Isaiah 55:8–9 declares: "For my thoughts are not your thoughts, neither are your ways my ways, says the LORD. For as the heavens are higher than the earth, so are my ways higher than your ways and my thoughts than your thoughts."[152]

This statement of God's superior modes of thinking calls on man to adopt a different type of conceptual framework when examining matters that involve or affect man's relationship to God. This chapter discusses the eternal significance of three such matters—faith, love, and sin—as they relate to man's ultimate fate.

Following original sin, every person comes into existence in a fallen state, spiritually separated from God.[153] Because sin constitutes a timeless injustice of divine consequence, it merits a correspondingly timeless penalty. Death is this penalty, and it is eternal by its very nature.[154] As a result, even though the progeny of

Adam and Eve are not the root cause of the injustice that resulted in them inheriting a sinful nature, they are, nonetheless, sinful beings who are subject to the eternal penalty for sin.

The permanence of death is overcome by the redemptive suffering of Jesus Christ, who is the only sinless member of the human race. Because the Son of man is a timeless being[155] who does not deserve to suffer death, his voluntary submission to death on behalf of mankind has the effect of annulling the permanence of this penalty for fallen humanity. Phrased another way, because Christ is a sinless, infinite being, his willing submission to death on behalf of sinful mankind nullifies the infiniteness of the penalty for man's evil. With divine justice satisfied with respect to this issue, the faithful can be redeemed to a sinless, timeless existence following the termination of their sinful, temporal lives.

According to First Peter 1:20, this plan of redemption was established "before the foundation of the world."[156] Because this plan was established "from all eternity,"[157] it is foretold in numerous ways in the Old Testament. The *Catechism* states, "The coming of God's Son to earth is an event of such immensity that God willed to prepare for it over centuries."[158] Within the nation of Israel, chosen to host the redeemer of all mankind,[159] God "makes everything converge on Christ: all the rituals and sacrifices, figures and symbols of the 'First Covenant.'"[160] Entire books have been written on the various Old Testament passages that presage Christ. Because of this, only three will be mentioned here.

First, God's act of sacrificing his long-awaited only Son for the sake of sinful mankind was prefigured in the account of Abraham's willingness to sacrifice his long-awaited only son, Isaac, for the sake of God in Genesis 22. The fact that this account appears in the very first book of the Bible signifies that God had established his plan of redemption from the beginning.

Another auguring of Christ appears in Psalm 22:7–18. This passage is notable for its specificity, reading like an eye-witness account of Christ's crucifixion even though it was written many generations before the events it describes: "All who see me mock at me, they make mouths at me, they wag their heads; 'He committed his cause to the LORD; let him deliver him, let him rescue him, for he delights in him!' …dogs are round about me; a company of evildoers encircle me; they have pierced my hands and feet—I can count all my bones—they stare and gloat over me; they divide my garments among them, and for my clothing they cast lots."[161]

Isaiah 53:2–11 is an exceptionally detailed prediction of Christ,[162] describing his humility, telling of his life of nonviolence and complete lack of deceitfulness,[163] foretelling his trial before the Sanhedrin when he refused to respond to the obviously false, conflicting testimony of his accusers,[164] describing his execution by crucifixion,[165] spelling out the purpose of his sacrifice,[166] predicting he would be laid to rest in a rich man's tomb[167] despite being put to death alongside criminals,[168] and prophesying his resurrection to life following his passion:[169]

> He was despised and rejected by men; a man of sorrows, and acquainted with grief; and as one from whom men hide their faces he was despised, and we esteemed him not.
>
> Surely he has borne our griefs and carried our sorrows; yet we esteemed him stricken, struck down by God, and afflicted.
>
> But he was wounded for our transgressions, he was bruised for our iniquities; upon him was the

chastisement that made us whole, and with his stripes we are healed.

All we like sheep have gone astray; we have turned every one to his own way; and the Lord has laid on him the iniquity of us all.

He was oppressed, and he was afflicted, yet he opened not his mouth; like a lamb that is led to the slaughter, and like a sheep that before its shearers is silent, so he opened not his mouth.

By oppression and judgment he was taken away; and as for his generation, who considered that he was cut off out of the land of the living, stricken for the transgression of my people?

And they made his grave with the wicked and with a rich man in his death, although he had done no violence, and there was no deceit in his mouth.

Yet it was the will of the Lord to bruise him; he has put him to grief; when he makes himself an offering for sin, he shall see his offspring, he shall prolong his days; the will of the Lord shall prosper in his hand; he shall see the fruit of the travail of his soul and be satisfied; by his knowledge shall the righteous one, my servant, make many to be accounted righteous; and he shall bear their iniquities.[170]

When Christ arrives into human history, he is given a name that is perfectly suited to both his mission and his nature as a being: "Jesus," which means "God saves" in Hebrew.[171] More specifically, the name "Jesus"—or *Yehshua* in Hebrew —means "Yahweh is salvation."[172] "Yahweh" is a transliteration of the ineffable Hebrew name for God, *YHWH,* which is derived from the Hebrew word for "I Am," *e'heyeh.*[173] "I Am" conveys the timelessness and absoluteness of God, and is the name by which God revealed himself to Moses in Exodus 3:14–15. The name "Jesus" can thus be translated to English more literally as, "I Am is salvation" or "I Am saves." The name "Jesus" therefore "signifies that the very name of God is present in the person of his Son."[174]

To understand the nature of the salvation provided by this remarkable individual named "I Am saves," it is necessary to further explore the makeup of God as a being, as well as the place redeemed mankind is to have in God as "partakers of the divine nature."[175] For this, one must understand not only the composition of the Trinity, but also the mechanics of the Trinity.

The discussion of the Trinity in the first chapter of Part II includes a description of the relationship that exists between the three persons of the divine being, with each person engaging in all the reciprocities of faith and selflessness required for the experience of love. To review, the love between these three persons is so perfect, so total, that it forms a single unified being—the being called "God." God, therefore, is literally the personification of love; God's very being is love itself.[176]

Recalling the first prerequisite of love from the discussion in Part I, which states that love cannot occur without the existence of two or more persons, it should now be clear that it would be contradictory to declare that "God is love,"[177] yet he somehow does not consist of anything more than one person. Love cannot occur without two or more persons, a fact that can easily be verified through personal experience. This fact of love applies to God's very being. "God is love" only because God is a Trinity of persons. God could not be love itself if he did not consist of more than one person.

Recognizing that love requires more than one person, and recognizing further that God is a Trinity of persons, consider what Jesus said in John 14:6 about his role in the Trinity: "I am the way, and the truth, and the life; no one comes to the Father, but by me."[178] When Christ declares that no one comes to the Father except through him, this assertion can and should be understood in a literalist, mechanistic manner.

Christ is the begotten Son of both God and man. As such, he is the fusion of the Creator and the created. As the *Catechism* states, "Through his very bodily condition he sums up in himself the elements of the material world."[179] In the Trinity, Christ unites to the Father and to the Holy Spirit in perfect love. Through this unification, the Creator is joined in love to that which has been created, thereby bringing man, who is a created being, into a love-based unity of being with God. Jesus, by virtue of the fact that he is fully man and fully divine, is therefore the means through which fallen humanity is brought into a loving union with the Trinity.[180]

In John 17:20–23, Jesus describes the manner in which he brings man into the Trinitarian structure: "I do not pray for these only, but also for those who believe in me through their word, that they may all be one; even as you, Father, are in me, and I in you, that they also may be in us, so that the world may believe that you have sent me. The glory which you have given me I have given to them, that they may be one even as we are one, *I in them and you in me, that they may become perfectly one.*" [Emphasis added.][181]

This description of the mechanics of divine love conveys that, through Christ, redeemed man will join to God in a loving society in which each individual, like the three persons of the Trinity, maintains a distinct and separate personhood from the others, while sharing in an experience of perfect love with all others. In this experience of perfect love, the faithful become unified to God's very being.

The Apostle Paul describes this unification to the very being of God in First Corinthians 12:12–26 when he states that redeemed man will become "one body" with God.[182] In First Corinthians 15:28, Paul writes that, in the eternal state, God becomes "all in all"[183]—that is, God lives fully in man in love, and man lives fully in God in love.[184] In Romans 11:11–24, redeemed man is described as a "branch" that is grafted onto the "root" (the "root" being an analogy for God).[185] Second Peter 1:4 states that through Christ redeemed men and women become "partakers of the divine nature."[186] Revelation 21:9 uses the language of marriage to refer to the fusion of redeemed mankind to God, calling them "the Bride, the wife of the Lamb."[187] Matthew 22:4 likewise uses the institution of marriage as an analogy to describe the point of man's unification to God in love, referring to it as a "marriage feast."[188]

The *Catechism* describes this same concept by quoting the theologian Saint Athanasius of Alexandria: "For the Son of God became man so that we might become God."[189] The *Catechism* also quotes Saint Thomas Aquinas: "The only-begotten Son of God, wanting to make us sharers in his divinity, assumed our nature, so that he, made man, might make men gods."[190] The *Catechism* further states: "This communion of life and love with the Trinity... is called 'heaven.'"[191] In a word, it is "salvation."

To summarize, Jesus is the means through which man is able to enter into a loving union with God because Jesus is the fusion of man and God in one person, joined to the Father and to the Holy Spirit in love through perfect faith and selflessness. Man's faith is necessary for salvation because faith is an indispensable prerequisite for the existence of relational love, including love between man and God.[192] When these concepts are put together, it means that it is only through Jesus Christ that the body of faithful mankind is brought into a loving union with God.

The role and importance of faith in man's salvation should now be clear, but it is worth emphasizing yet again that faith is the *only* way man can attain salvation because faith is the only way a person can experience love with God. Because of this, the necessity of faith is a point made over and over again in the Bible. Hebrews 11:6 declares, "without faith it is impossible to please him. For whoever would draw near to God must believe that he exists and that he rewards those who seek him."[193] In Romans 16:26, Paul speaks of the "obedience of faith"[194] as man's first obligation.[195] In John 3:18, Jesus states explicitly, "He who believes in him is not condemned; he who does not believe is condemned already."[196]

As with Christ's assertion in John 14:6 that he is "the way, and the truth, and the life,"[197] Christ's declaration of condemnation for the faithless in John 3:18 and similar passages should be taken literally. In Luke 9:35, God the Father beseeches man to pay careful attention to the teachings of Jesus, saying of him, "This is my Son, my Chosen, listen to him!"[198] In Matthew 25:30, Jesus warns of the existence of an "outer darkness, where there will be weeping and gnashing of teeth."[199]

According to the *Catechism*, this realm can be described as a "state of definitive self-exclusion from communion with God."[200] It "consists of eternal separation from God in whom alone man can have the life and happiness for which he was created and for which he longs."[201] The *Catechism* further instructs that "there is no repentance for men after death."[202] Together, these teachings raise an immensely important piece of the problem of pain—the problem of eternal suffering, otherwise known as the problem of hell.

After the conclusion of man's temporal life, man enters into a timeless state of being similar to that experienced by Adam and Eve at the outset of their existence.[203] As described in the preceding paragraphs, this state of timeless being is either spent in communion with God or separated from him. The anguish of those who exist in a state of timeless separation from God is so profound that, in Matthew 18:9, Jesus declares, "And if your eye causes you to sin, pluck it out and throw it from you; it is better for you to enter life with one eye than with two eyes to be thrown into the hell of fire."[204]

Assuming Jesus's assertions in Matthew 18:9 and similar passages are true, the suffering that man experiences in his present state pales in comparison to the sorrow and misery experienced by those destined to live in eternal separation from God. If God really is all-loving and all-powerful, what possible explanation could be given for such suffering?

Once again, the key insights are to be found in the prerequisites of relational love. If a sinful person is faithless at the point when he receives *certain* knowledge of both God's existence and omnibenevolence, this newfound knowledge will itself preclude that person from being able to establish the faith necessary to enter into a loving relationship with God. *Faith, by definition, requires the absence of certainty.* Because faith is a prerequisite of love, faithless fallen beings cease to have the ability to experience love with God once they acquire sure knowledge of God's existence and absolute goodness.

In order to acquire sure knowledge of God's absolute goodness, a creature must possess knowledge of good and evil. Creatures who possess certain knowledge of God's existence but lack the capacity to understand God's absolute goodness, like Adam and Eve prior to their acquisition of knowledge of good and evil, are creatures who have the ability not only to exercise faith toward

God, but also the ability to grow that faith. In a fallen state of existence, man is able to establish and grow his faith in God, as well as his faith in other people, due to a similar dynamic.

Just as Adam and Eve had knowledge of God's existence by virtue of their personal interactions with him, fallen man has knowledge of the existence of other people by virtue of his interactions with them. Prior to the fall, the first humans' faith in God was capable of both growth and diminution because Adam and Eve lacked knowledge of good and evil, which precluded them from knowing that God is absolutely good.[205] Similarly, fallen man is able to place, increase, lessen, and lose faith in other people because his awareness of good and evil enables him to know that other people are prone to commit acts of sin, a fact that prevents anyone from knowing whether another person will reciprocate a given act of kindness.

Because of fallen humanity's current separation from God, fallen man likewise possesses the ability to place, grow, decrease, and abandon faith in God. However, after fallen man's temporal life ends, he will acquire *certain* knowledge of God's existence. By virtue of fallen humanity's knowledge of good and evil, man will also acquire *certain* knowledge of God's all-loving nature. Because faith is a prerequisite of love, and because faith cannot be developed in the face of certainty, a faithless person who possesses certain knowledge of both God's existence and omnibenevolence no longer has the ability to experience love with God. For this reason, it is logically impossible for there to be repentance for men after death.

The prerequisites of love also provide the key insights necessary to understand the reason for the eternal suffering of fallen angels, which constitutes another facet of the problem of hell.[206] Unlike fallen man, who enters into existence in a fallen state due to the sinful decision-making of the first two humans, passages such as Isaiah 14:12–14[207] and Jude 1:6[208] indicate that angels entered into existence in an unfallen state. Genesis 3:22 reveals that angels have knowledge of God's absolute goodness when it states that, as a result of man's original sin, "man has become like one of us, knowing good and evil."[209] (The "us" in Genesis 3:22 is best understood as a reference to the angelic beings who coexist with God in the eternal realm.[210])

Because "God is love,"[211] when an unfallen angelic being who possesses *certain* knowledge of both God's existence and omnibenevolence willfully breaks faith with God by choosing sin over love, that being has deliberately rejected love itself; it has purposefully rejected that which it *knows* to be the very essence of what God is as a being. By purposefully and knowingly giving themselves over to the antithesis of love while existing in a timeless state of being, fallen angels intentionally chose to make themselves forever incapable of experiencing love with God. As such, they made an affirmative decision to make themselves unredeemable.

There is nothing unjust or unloving about the lack of repentance for angelic beings who knowingly rejected love with God through their willful adoption of sin. It could be argued, though, that the same lack of repentance would not apply to human beings because fallen humanity cannot be certain of God's existence. Surely, according to this argument, an all-loving God would never condemn people to eternal separation from him when they could not even be certain of his existence.[212] But this argument is specious if:

(1)   Every person is created with a timeless, eternal soul[213] for the purpose of allowing that person to join to God in a timeless loving union.[214] (Man's immortal spirit is the final way in which he shares

in the "likeness" of the Trinitarian God, who is the union of Father, Son, and Holy Spirit.)

(2) "Heaven" consists of the actualization of man's time-less loving union with God.[215]

(3) Faith is a prerequisite for the experience of love. As a result, a loving union between man and God cannot occur in the absence of faith from either party.[216]

If these statements are true, then eternal separation from God for faithless individuals does not constitute an unloving act. Individuals who believe in God but who nonetheless willfully favor their own self-centered ends over love with God will likewise experience eternal separation from him; this does not constitute an unloving act either. Just as an adulterer compromises a marital union by acting on a selfish desire for sex with someone other than his spouse, the inclusion of even one individual who willfully favors his own self-centered ends over love would compromise the experience of perfect love for God and everyone else who is joined to him. For this reason, neither faithlessness nor self-centeredness can have any place in an eternal loving union with God.

If it is apparent that faithlessness and self-centeredness can have no place in a perfect, loving union with God, it should be all the more evident that individuals who willfully desire to harm others can have no place in this union either. There is nothing conceptually difficult about the idea that a hate-filled, unrepentant murderer would be excluded from an eternal loving union with God. Were God to unify himself to such a person, that individual would exercise his free will to undermine love. As First John 3:15

states, "All who hate a brother or sister are murderers, and you know that murderers do not have eternal life abiding in them."[217]

The example of a hate-filled, unrepentant murderer should make it obvious that the existence of an "outer darkness" does not in any way contradict God's omnibenevolent nature. Again, if:

(1)　Man has been made as a timeless being for the purpose of joining to God in a timeless loving union, and if

(2)　Love cannot occur unless everyone in the relationship has faith in one another and is willing to disavow the pursuit of selfish ends which can only be acquired at the expense of others in the relationship, then

(3)　The existence of a realm of faithless, hateful, and unapologetically sinful timeless beings who are eternally separated from God is logically necessary in order for timeless love to exist between God and individuals who do have faith and who repent of their sins.

Some may counter that, if an all-loving and all-powerful God actually existed as described above, he would mercifully extinguish from existence those beings who cannot join to him in a timeless loving union due to their lack of faith. To not do so, according to this argument, would be unloving because it would force beings to suffer the torment of having to live forever with the realization that they have permanently forfeited the whole purpose of their existence. In other words, hell is an unnecessary

cruelty. Accordingly, the existence of an eternal hell and an omnibenevolent, omnipotent God are held to be contradictory.

But this argument ignores the first and most obvious prerequisite of love: the existence of two or more beings. As noted in Part
I, it is self-evident that man's temporal existence is a necessary
precondition for him to be able to experience love during his
earthly life. Just as temporal existence is a precondition for the
experience of love in a time-based setting, timeless existence is
a precondition for the experience of love in a timeless setting. *A
person must exist as an eternal being in order to have the ability to enter
into a timeless loving relationship with the eternal God.*[218]

If God's reason for creating man with an immortal soul is
to enable man to experience timeless love with God, then God's
creation of man as an eternal being constitutes an act of love.
But this act of love in no way precludes the existence of hell, for
the simple reason that eternal being—by definition—leaves no
alternative but for beings to always exist somewhere. Consequently,
if a timeless being has excluded himself from a timeless loving
union with God due to the absence of faith, that being continues
to exist, albeit separated from God. Eternal separation from God
is thus the inevitable endpoint for faithless timeless beings who
acquire certain knowledge of both God's existence and omnibenevolence. For these reasons, the existence of hell is in no way a
contradiction of God's all-loving nature.

Eternal separation from God does not contradict God's perfectly just nature either, because it is the separated individuals'
own lack of faith that is the cause of their inability to enter into
an eternal loving relationship with God. By refusing to entrust
themselves to God at any level, such persons are making a decision to withhold the key element that is necessary for love to be
established between themselves and God. In essence, it is a choice

of self over God; it is a rejection of a loving relationship with God through the refusal to place any amount of trust in him.

This rejection may take the form of indifference to God, or it may be an affirmative determination that God does not exist. In other cases, the refusal to place trust in God may stem from indecisiveness. A person questions and weighs whether belief is sensible but remains unwilling to place any amount of faith in God. In all these cases, the fundamental choice of the individual is the same: a refusal to place trust in God. This is a self-enclosing, self-isolating choice; it is a forswearing of any degree of openness to God, which can only occur by placing faith in him.[219] In sum, it is the opposite of love, which is giving of itself, hopeful, believing, and desirous of connection.

As described in First Corinthians 13:4–7, love is not indifferent, it is not untrusting, and it is not closed in upon itself or otherwise selfishly consumed with itself.[220] God is none of these, but people are free to choose to be any or all of them. Without such freedom, love would not be possible. When a person freely chooses to be indifferent, faithless, or selfishly closed in upon himself with respect to his relationship with God, it is the person who has barricaded himself from God, not the other way around.

Just as a person denies himself love during his temporal life by refusing to reciprocate faith that others extend to him, an individual denies himself love with God through a similar withholding of faith. Justice is in no way compromised by God disassociating himself from such an individual. Through that person's own distrust, his own unwillingness to place faith even as tiny as a mustard seed in God, he has confined himself to his own being.

The assertion that faith as miniscule as a mustard seed is sufficient for salvation is drawn from Christ's statement in Matthew 17:20: "I say to you, if you have faith the size of a mustard seed, you will say to this mountain, 'Move from here to there,' and it will move. Nothing will be impossible for you."[221] This statement arose in the context of Jesus's disciples being unable to drive out an evil spirit from a child, but the message of Matthew 17:14–20 can be construed more broadly as a statement of the level of faith that is needed to make a person whole through the removal of the spirit of evil which resides within him. Faith in God as minute as a mustard seed is enough for God to remove the evil within a child of God and restore that person to the proper state of being.

When a person who has thus been freed from sin is joined to God in the eternal state, truly nothing will be impossible for him. The reason nothing will be impossible for him is because he will exist in a transcendent, godlike state of being similar to that of Adam and Eve prior to the fall. As described in the first chapter of Part II, this state of being is categorically different from the sinful state of existence currently experienced by man.

In order for man to be transformed from his current state of sinfulness to a transcendent state of existence similar to that which was experienced by Adam and Eve before the fall, man must be completely freed from sin. The act of freeing man from sin is described in First Corinthians 3:13–15 as a purifying fire that will commence on the day of judgment, consuming every work of man that was carried out with sinful intent.[222] Isaiah 65:17 states that, after every last facet of sin is consumed, "the former things shall not be remembered or come to mind."[223]

Freed from sin, the faithful will then enter into the experience of perfect love with God. However, those without faith in God will be left with "neither root nor branch" following God's fiery annihilation of sin.[224] Having never developed a single faith-based offshoot from their beings that enables them to join to God in love,[225] the faithless will remain forever separated from God in the "outer darkness" referenced by Christ in Matthew 8:12.[226]

Of course, the eternal separation of the faithless in the "outer darkness" is not the only biblical description of their fate. Matthew 3:12 declares that the condemned will be subjected to "unquenchable fire" in the eternal state.[227] Matthew 18:8 also references this endless burning, calling it an "eternal fire."[228] It is referenced again in Mark 9:43, where it is once more described as an "unquenchable fire."[229] In Revelation, the location where the condemned will be pooled together for eternity is called the "lake of fire."[230] How can the existence of such eternal burning be logically reconciled with the existence of a perfectly loving God?

The answer is straightforward. As a result of their refusal to place faith in God prior to acquiring certain knowledge of God's existence and omnibenevolence, these eternal beings have become forever faithless. As discussed earlier in this chapter, faithlessness is the opposite of love. Anything that is opposed to love is sin. This means that the very beings of the faithless have become manifestations of sin in a timeless form. Consequently, the same fire that is employed by God on the day of judgment to free the faithful from their sin will indefinitely consume those who have become timeless beings of sin by virtue of their faithlessness. *God's fiery consumption of that which is the opposite of love cannot logically be regarded as unloving.*

Some may object that, if God were actually all-loving, he would only apply this terrifying fire to the faithful, thereby freeing them from sin while sparing the faithless from the experience of eternal burning. This objection fails for a combination of two reasons. First, because God is perfectly just, his justice will be imposed in an absolute manner; no sin will be exempt from the flames. Second, the claim that God would make exceptions for certain forms of sin fails to take account of the implications of Genesis 1–3.

As described in the opening chapter of Part II, by committing original sin, the first humans pulled themselves and their entire domain out of a timeless state of existence, transforming it into a time-based existence. Upon man being restored to a state where he again "inhabits eternity" with God,[231] anything that remains of the temporal realm will be omnipresent to man, in the same manner as it is to God.[232]

To better understand the practical realities of this, it is necessary to explore the meaning of "omnipresence" in greater detail. The concept of omnipresence is closely tied to the assertion in Isaiah 57:15 that God "inhabits eternity."[233] This phrase was briefly examined in the opening chapter of Part II, but it is worth revisiting—albeit from a slightly different angle than before—because it is such a remarkably peculiar way to describe the nature of eternal existence.

To "inhabit eternity" indicates that eternal existence does not consist of living forever within an endless march of time. Instead, eternity is somehow "inhabited" or "occupied." Though there is no way for fallen mankind to fully grasp what this entails, it is clear that "inhabiting eternity" cannot mean that God is trapped within the one-directional flow of linear time. If he were, God could not know the future, a concept which contradicts the entire basis of biblical prophecy. To "inhabit eternity" must therefore refer to some form of omnipresence. At a minimum, it suggests a type of existence in which the entire span of temporal history is continually present before God.[234] As the *Catechism* states, "To God, all moments are present in their immediacy."[235]

Numerous biblical passages—including Proverbs 26:26, Matthew 10:26, Mark 4:22, Luke 8:17 and 12:2–3, and First Corinthians 4:5—indicate that every human being will likewise have a comprehensive view of temporal history when all of humanity is assembled together before God on the day of judgment.[236] Specifically, these passages indicate that everything that every person has ever done, along with all of the unseen motives for every action that everyone took during their temporal lives, will become known to everyone on the day of judgment. It is inconceivable how anyone could become aware of such a staggering volume of information in the absence of occupying some form of omnipresent existence.

As has already been discussed at length, man was made in the "likeness" of God, who is eternal. Part of what this means is that man was made to inhabit eternity in a manner like that of God himself. Wisdom 2:23 makes this plain when it states, "God created man…in the image of his own eternity."[237] On the day of judgment, when all of mankind "inhabits eternity" in the direct presence of God, every person will experience omnipresence in the same manner as God. At this point, but prior to God's deployment of the "fire" that consumes all sin, everyone will have total knowledge of everything that transpired within the temporal realm.

This means that every lie, fraud, rape, murder, act of torture, adulterous affair, and cruelty will be made manifest to all. As long as this shameful array of evil remains unconsumed by purifying fire, it will remain continually before everyone, as it is for God. The omnipresence of *any* of this sin would undoubtedly undermine redeemed man's experience of love in some way or another.

Because of this, the destruction of sin on the day of judgment will be all-encompassing. Because time itself is a direct consequence of original sin, the destruction of sin will include the destruction of the entire space-time universe. This is made clear in Second Peter 3:7–10, which states, "the heavens and earth that now exist have been stored up for fire, being kept until the day of judgment…then the elements will be dissolved with fire, and the earth and the works that are upon it will be burned up."[238]

First Corinthians 3:13 states that "the fire will test what sort of work each one has done."[239] If an act was carried out for a sinful purpose, it will burn, and its destruction will be total. Indeed, the erasure of man's sins will be so total that, according to Hebrews 8:12, it will wipe out even God's memory of it: "I will remember their sins no more."[240] The only acts that will survive will be those that were carried out for a sinless purpose, without dishonesty or other immoral ulterior motives. These works alone will continually remain before everyone in the final state of existence.

Referencing this final state, Jesus describes a reversal in the status of various people: "some are last who will be first, and some are first who will be last."[241] Thus, some who were poor and held in low esteem in the temporal world will enter eternity with a lifetime of works that survive the flames of final judgment. Others who were lauded for their successful efforts to accumulate wealth, power, and fame during their temporal lives will witness their works consumed by fire on the day of judgment, leaving them destitute of "treasures in heaven."[242] There will be yet others whose sinful works netted them practically nothing of value during their temporal lives, but even what little they have will be taken away because they too lived lives bereft of sinless deeds: "but from the one who has not, even what he has will be taken away."[243]

Following this total destruction of sin by fire, Isaiah 65:17 states that all of temporal existence will then be replaced by "new heavens and a new earth."[244] This same event is briefly described in Matthew 19:28 when Jesus references "the renewal of all things."[245] It is described yet again in Acts 3:21 as "the time of universal restoration that God announced long ago through his holy prophets."[246] It is referenced in Second Peter 3:13 as a "new heavens and a new earth in which righteousness dwells."[247] Revelation 21:5 states that "all things" will be made "new."[248]

This biblical language paints a picture of the restoration of physical creation *in its entirety* to a state similar to that inhabited by Adam and Eve prior to the fall. As explained in the opening chapter of Part II, this state of existence is not time-based. It is a state of timelessness that is totally devoid of selfishness, indifference, suffering, and death.[249]

In this restored creation, the creatures placed under man's "dominion"[250] will exist and behave as they did in their original states. Thus, instead of an ecosystem that stays in balance due to the ruthlessly self-centered, competitive actions of all forms of life, it will be an ecosystem that stays in balance due to the unfailingly selfless, giving actions of all life forms. Literally *every* form of life—from the very simplest to the most complex—will operate in the opposite manner it does now. Collectively, they will form a vast and staggeringly diverse network of selfless life, all innately acting in the service of one another, presided over by sinless man.

Such a system of creation is nearly inconceivable to fallen man because it represents a wholesale reversal of the manner in which all life is ordered in the temporal realm. But it is precisely what is described by the prophet Isaiah: "The wolf shall dwell with the lamb, and the leopard shall lie down with the kid, and the calf and the lion and the fatling together, and a little child shall lead them. The cow and the bear shall feed; their young shall lie down together; and the lion shall eat straw like the ox…. They shall not hurt or destroy in all my holy mountain; for the earth shall be full of the knowledge of the LORD as the waters cover the sea."[251]

In addition to the restoration of the various life forms placed under man's dominion, the material realm itself will cease to be governed by laws that are indifferent to the will of man. In a fallen realm governed by self-centeredness and indifference to others, the material realm must follow immutable rules in order for love to be possible. C. S. Lewis explains why this is the case: "If a 'world' or material system had only a single inhabitant it might conform at every moment to his wishes—'trees for his sake would crowd into a shade'. But if you were introduced into a world which thus varied at my every whim, you would be quite unable to act in it and would thus lose the exercise of your free will."[252]

While such variance of the material realm obviously would be untenable in a world populated by selfish beings, C. S. Lewis's analysis does not apply to an unfallen realm. In an unfallen realm governed by universal selflessness, there is no need for the material order to be governed by fixed rules because no one will exercise command over the material realm in a manner that will undermine love. This explains Christ's statement in Matthew 17:20 concerning the power of sinless man over the material order in the eternal state: "you will say to this mountain, 'Move from here to there,' and it will move. Nothing will be impossible for you."[253]

In order to make way for this restoration of physical creation, the temporal realm must be obliterated. As stated in Second Peter 3:7–13, the annihilation of the temporal realm will take place on the day of judgment when God deploys a "fire" that will consume the entire space-time universe, along with all sin within it.[254] As God's purifying fire is applied to *all* sin, those who have become sin in a timeless form will themselves ignite.[255] Because they have become eternal beings of sin, the burning will never cease. As horrific as this fate may be, God's treatment of timeless sinful beings in this manner does not constitute an unloving act because sin is—by its very nature—the *opposite* of love.

God's treatment of sinful beings in this manner does not constitute an unjust act either, because perfect justice—by its very nature—*requires* that sin be punished with its rightful penalty.[256] Because sin undermines the whole purpose of life, death is the rightful punishment for sin.[257] Because separation from the Source of life[258] constitutes a form of death,[259] when the faithless are forever banished from the presence of God after appearing before him on the day of judgment, Revelation 21:8 refers to this act of banishment as "the second death."[260] Now separated from

God in the "outer darkness" of the afterlife, these timeless beings of sin will remain forever trapped by the combination of their eternal existence and the fire that justly consumes sin.[261]

In contrast to its effects on the faithless, the fire of final judgment will operate to the benefit of the faithful, serving to free them from every last vestige of sin. At the conclusion of this purgative fire, every sin that was committed in the temporal world will be completely erased from existence, along with all memory of the suffering and death that are the consequence of sin: "death shall be no more, neither shall there be mourning nor crying nor pain any more, for the former things have passed away."[262]

With all memory of sin, suffering, and death completely burned away, the closing verse of Isaiah declares that the faithful—who are now in a state of pure sinlessness—will then look upon the unredeemed and be utterly repulsed by what they see: "And they shall go forth and look on the dead bodies of the men that have rebelled against me; for their worm shall not die, their fire shall not be quenched, and they shall be an abhorrence to all flesh."[263]

Faced with the grotesque reality of sin and seeing with their own eyes the horrific eternal consequences of giving oneself over to it, sinless man will never again be seduced by it. Sin will be nothing but an "abhorrence" to the faithful because they will have now viewed it from the same perspective as God—a being who is totally sinless, possesses knowledge of good and evil, and understands the transformative effects of sin at the most fundamental level of being.[264]

For those who ask why God did not provide man and angels with all this knowledge at the outset of their existence, the answer is that both groups needed to have the ability to establish faith in God through the free exercise of their will. Faith cannot be established unless an individual makes a decision to trust God in spite of the risk that he may incur tangible loss as a result.

Isaiah 14:12–14, for example, reveals that the most powerful angel thought that if he stayed faithful to God, he would be deprived of the ability to supplant God in the hierarchy of beings. This angel decided that the pursuit of this self-centered objective was more important than the continuance of his loving relationship with God: "You said in your heart, 'I will ascend to heaven; above the stars of God I will set my throne on high; I will sit on the mount of assembly in the far north; I will ascend above the heights of the clouds, I will make myself like the Most High.'"[265]

In the case of Adam and Eve, the exercise of faith required them to be willing to forego the acquisition of knowledge of good and evil. Like the fallen angels, they too decided to value a self-centered objective over their loving relationship with God.

As these examples illustrate, an individual's faith must be sincere enough that he is willing to incur actual loss if he is wrong about prioritizing his loving relationship with God over a given self-centered end. Because authentic faith requires a true willingness to self-sacrifice for the sake of the beloved, the exercise of faith is neither meaningless nor trivial.[266] On the contrary, courage is required to exercise one's will in this manner.

Only after an individual's faith is securely established through the free exercise of his will can God's full knowledge be shared with that individual without love being compromised. Redeemed man will acquire this full knowledge when, in a state of sinlessness, he looks upon the condemned and sees with absolute certainty that faithlessness and self-centeredness are nothing but a self-destructive "abhorrence." At that moment, it will be perfectly clear that sin is a decision of such immense importance that it literally transforms an individual at the most fundamental level of being, causing him to view all of existence from an untrusting, self-centered perspective.

Recognizing the wholly transformative effects of sin and knowing the irreversible nature of this transformation when sin is committed by a timeless being who possesses full knowledge of God,[267] when the redeemed look upon the condemned following the fire of final judgment, they will be horrified by what they see and will want no part of it, ever.

Turning away from the abhorrent sight of these unloving beings, the faithful will spend eternity selflessly serving God[268] and the "great multitude...from every nation"[269] who are forever wedded to God as members of "one body."[270] With the Trinity now vastly expanded to encompass this great multitude of "divinized" beings,[271] and with every member of this body faithfully exercising his godlike power in the service of the others, the redeemed will experience the inexpressible joy that results from their wholly loving relationship with God and one another, forever.[272]

In summary, because God is all-loving, he makes man as an eternal being for the sake of allowing man and God to enter into a timeless loving union with one another. Because faith is a precondition of love, faithlessness undermines man's ability to experience timeless love with God. Anything that undermines love is sin. Because divine justice dictates that all sin ultimately be consumed as part of God's loving restoration of man's fallen realm, and because it is not unloving to impose this form of justice on that which is by definition unloving, God's application of fire to those who have become timeless beings of sin through their faithlessness is an act that is logically compatible with the assertions that God is all-loving, all-just, all-wise, and all-powerful.

THE SUFFICIENCY
OF FAITH

One matter remains. Is faith the only requirement a person must meet for salvation, or is something more required of individuals as well? This question is of critical importance because the task of reconciling the existence of eternal suffering with a perfectly just and all-loving God becomes more difficult if a person's salvation is contingent on anything beyond that individual's own faith, together with God's grace.[273] The following facets of this question will be considered:

(1) Are both faith and works necessary for salvation, or is faith alone sufficient?

(2) Is the eternal fate of individuals the product of God's predestination, or is it the product of their own freely made faith-based decision-making?

(3) Is a person's salvation dependent to some degree on his reasoning abilities, or is it ultimately only contingent on faith?

(4)   Is there a minimum duration of time that a person
       must exist in the temporal world in order to have ad-
       equate opportunity to make the faith-based decision
       that will determine his eternal fate? Said differently,
       is salvation contingent on both time and faith, or
       faith alone?

These four items obviously do not represent an exhaustive list
of issues that have been or could be raised concerning the broader
question of whether faith alone is sufficient for salvation. People
have claimed that salvation is forfeited for all kinds of reasons,
including the decision not to join a specific religious group, the
failure to perform certain rituals, or a refusal to proclaim fealty
to a specific clerical authority. Because resources already exist
that address these and similar claims, they are not discussed here.

Faith and Works

The "faith versus works" question is frequently raised in discussions of salvation. The position taken in this book is that faith is
the key to salvation; works are evidence of faith. The former half of
this statement is supported by Romans 11:6, Ephesians 2:8–9, Titus
3:5, and similar passages;[274] the latter half is supported by James
2:17, which reads, "faith by itself, if it has no works, is dead."[275]

In other words, anyone who truly believes in Christ's salvation will feel compelled to produce "good fruit" according to his
ability.[276] Such works are the inevitable manifestation of genuine
faith because a person's works—the things for which he sacrifices
and strives—have their origin in his most deeply held beliefs.

Those who truly believe in God and desire communion with
him will be motivated to perform good works. In contrast, those
who do not truly believe in God will only labor in furtherance
of finite, worldly ends. This is why Jesus declared, "you will know

them by their fruits."[277] The clearest evidence of a person's inmost desires and beliefs are the ends for which that person labors. A man without good works is therefore a man without genuine faith. If a person insists that he has faith but does not align *any* of his actions with his supposed belief, then he is lying about his belief, even if only to himself.

But just because works are the inevitable manifestation of genuine faith, it does not mean that works are the key to salvation. Suppose a man comes to sincere faith at the last instant of his life and therefore has no time to perform even a single work based on his new-found faith. Is this person destined to be eternally separated from God because death has arrived before he has performed a good work?

First Corinthians 3:15 indicates that some people will survive the flames of final judgment but their works will not: "If any man's work is burned up, he will suffer loss, though he himself will be saved, but only as through fire."[278] If there will be people who are saved even though none of their works survive the exacting test of final judgment, it follows that faith is the key to salvation.[279]

Predestination, Determinism, and Free Will

The second question concerns whether individuals are ultimately responsible for their eternal fate, or if God makes this decision for people. Certain language in the Bible, such as that referencing the "elect" of God,[280] can be interpreted to mean that God predestines some individuals for salvation and others for eternal separation.[281] This raises the following question: should the biblical language referencing the "elect" of God be interpreted in a manner that creates an irreconcilable conflict with passages like First Timothy 2:4, which states that God "desires all men to be saved,"[282] or is there a reasonable way of interpreting the word "elect" that does not create such a conflict?

To quote again from the *Catechism*: "To God, all moments of time are present in their immediacy. When therefore he establishes his eternal plan of 'predestination,' he includes in it each person's free response to his grace."[283] The *Catechism* goes on to explain, "God predestines no one to go to hell; for this, a willful turning away from God…is necessary, and persistence in it until the end."[284]

To paraphrase, God's omniscience enables him to know what each person's ultimate faith-based choice will be, and God's actions in the fallen world of man take into account the free-willed decision-making of each person. The use of words like "elect" in the Bible—which can be misconstrued to mean that God predestines only certain individuals to be saved—should instead be understood as a reference to the individuals whom God knows, by virtue of his omniscience, will be saved as a result of their own freely made faith-based decision-making.

But is it really the case that man is capable of making truly free decisions? One of the most recent academic figures to argue that man lacks this ability is Dr. Robert Sapolsky, a professor of neuroscience at Stanford University. In 2023, he published *Determined: A Science of Life Without Free Will*. As the title of this book indicates, Sapolsky is a "determinist," a person who believes that all events, including all human action, are determined by causes other than free will.

Sapolsky maintains that man is nothing more than a material being and further maintains that all matter adheres to immutable rules of physics. If both of these assertions are true, then every action a person takes is predetermined by the physical rules that govern the matter out of which that person and everything else in the universe are made. No one can do anything other than that which is already inevitable according to the complex web of rules that strictly govern how all matter operates. As Sapolsky declares,

"We are nothing more or less than the sum of that which we could not control—our biology, our environments, their interactions."[285]

This conclusion follows naturally from the faith-based presuppositions that underpin Sapolsky's worldview. In an October 2023 interview promoting his book, Sapolsky summarized these presuppositions and recounted the moment when he adopted them:

> Interviewer (Timothy Revell): Many of our listeners, they will know you as someone who spent years studying wild baboons... So, what made you decide to then suddenly look at free will so closely, which is, I guess, more often associated with philosophy? Was there, like, an enticing incident? Did something get you onto it first?

> Sapolsky: Yes. I turned fourteen years old, at one point, and had a somewhat existentially unnerving experience. And, that night, woke up at around two in the morning and said, "Aha, I get it. There's no God, there's no purpose, and there's no free will," and it's been kind of like that ever since.[286]

Assumptions drive conclusions. Neuroscience, like every other field of human study, begins with faith-based assumptions. If one assumes that no spiritual realm exists, and if one further assumes that all matter consistently follows immutable rules of physics, it follows that man has no free will. The reason for this conclusion is exceedingly simple: if man is nothing but a material being, then he is ultimately nothing more than an extremely complex physical machine, each and every component of which follows the immutable rules that govern matter, down to the very tiniest particle. If every physical particle in the universe consistently follows unvarying scientific laws of physics, to believe in free will would therefore seem to require one to believe that man can somehow willfully change the operation of one or more aspects of particle physics within his own being.

Because Sapolsky started with the assumption that there is nothing in existence other than the material realm, it is only logical for him to conclude that man has no free will. His reasoning has taken him exactly where his starting assumptions demanded—in a full circle, right back to the beliefs he adopted at age fourteen. As Sapolsky stated in a November 2023 podcast with the news media company *Vox*, "I was an adolescent when I decided there's no free will."[287]

The critical question, then, is not whether Sapolsky and other determinists have presented logical arguments to support their beliefs; it is whether they started their arguments with one or more incorrect assumptions. The most obvious way to answer this question is to ask what, if anything, man's experiences reveal about whether he has genuine free will. Is it not self-evident that man is free to make actual choices, even if many of these choices are constrained in various ways by a person's environment and physical state? Does experience really support the conclusion that everything man does is predetermined?

Any honest observer will conclude that man does in fact possess the capacity to freely make a considerable range of choices. Both faith and reasoning play an important role in many of these choices. This leads to the third question from the list above, which asks whether reasoning is a necessary precondition for man's salvation.

Faith and Reasoning

What happens to those who die without ever possessing the intellectual capacity to fully evaluate arguments for and against God?

The eternal fate of such persons is not directly addressed in the Bible. Assuming, for the sake of argument, that some of these individuals are destined for eternal separation from God, would this outcome not establish that God is unjust or unloving?

Nowhere in the Bible does Jesus or God the Father proclaim, "Your theological reasoning has saved you." Instead, in one interaction after another during his public ministry, Jesus makes it clear that salvation flows from faith. Christ's assertion in Luke 7:50 is typical of his teaching on this matter: "Your faith," he says to a woman known in the community as having lived a decidedly sinful life, "has saved you."[288]

As explained in Part I, reasoning begins with faith. Because of this, reasoning can enable one person to conclude that the existence of an omnipotent and omnibenevolent God is entirely compatible with observable reality, while enabling a second person with an equal level of education and intelligence to reach the exact opposite conclusion. The two sides can debate the merits of their respective positions ad nauseam, but all such arguments ultimately lead right back to where they began, with faith. Faith is the starting point of man's reasoning about God, as well as its end.

This is why the discussion of the philosophy of reasoning in Part I is so important to understand. It is critical to recognize that reasoning does not stand on its own. Faith-based assumptions *always* underlie reason. The failure to recognize that human reasoning ultimately rests on faith leads to the fallacy of thinking that everything in existence can eventually be understood through the application of analytical reasoning. More to the point, the failure to recognize that human reasoning ultimately rests on faith leads to the fallacy of thinking that, if God exists, analytical reasoning must be the way to reach him and understand him.

But this insistence on reasoning is in direct conflict with what the Bible teaches. The Bible instructs that the most important aspects of reality will remain hidden from those who are faithless. One must first believe in order to "know the secrets of the kingdom of heaven."[289] The *Catechism* summarizes the blinding effects of faithlessness as follows: "For those who stay on the 'outside,' everything remains enigmatic."[290]

The Bible's insistence on faith[291] can come as an affront to highly analytical people. One reason this is sometimes the case is because faith, unlike analytical reasoning, seems too easy, and anything so seemingly effortless is assumed to lack value. This assumption, which itself is based on faith, can lead highly analytical people to ridicule those who place faith in God. But the truly analytically minded person—the person who carefully examines the basis of his reasoning and refuses to succumb to intellectual dishonesty—will acknowledge that human reasoning ultimately rests on faith.

Faith's primacy over cold, calculating logic arises from the fact that faith, not reason, is the indispensable action necessary for the experience of relational love. Even the most educated, intelligent person on Earth cannot analyze his way to the experience of relational love. Because salvation consists of the experience of an eternal loving relationship between man and God, the decision to place faith in God is the act that determines whether a person enters into this relationship, not the act of engaging in reason-based analysis.

This does not mean that analytical reasoning cannot play a role in the salvation of particular individuals. Reasoning can and very frequently does have a crucial role in leading many people to belief in God. But it need not be so in all cases. Indeed, regardless of how much reasoning and analysis a person engages in, God will remain out of reach for that person unless he makes a choice to believe.

Faith and Time

If the choice to believe is the decisive factor that determines whether a person is saved, does the act of making this faith-based decision require a certain amount of time to perform? If so, then salvation is contingent on both faith and time. This issue is the focus of the fourth and final section of this chapter, which involves the relationship between faith, time, and timeless being.

Central to the overarching argument in this book is the assertion that the eternal realm operates in a manner that is categorically different from that of the temporal realm. Previous chapters have examined some of the ways that man's temporal mindset can frame his understanding of the nature of timeless existence, often leading him to inaccurately conceptualize foundational features of it.

Fallen man's struggle to accurately conceptualize the nature of timeless existence is a key reason man has difficulty understanding how the timeless soul goes about making its fundamental choice for or against God. Even though the inner workings of the soul will inevitably remain at least somewhat mysterious to man in his present state, the Bible provides enough information to allow several important conclusions to be made regarding the soul's capacities. This information is summarized in three short paragraphs below, then analyzed.

First, Genesis 1–3 indicates that God made man with the ability to choose between love and sin. If man has the ability to choose, then man has free will.

Second, Hebrews 11:6 is unequivocal that "without faith it is impossible to please God."[292] If it is in fact *impossible* to please God without faith, then no one is exempted from this requirement, not even those who experience a temporal life lasting for only a fraction of a second.

Third, in Deuteronomy 32:39 and Isaiah 43:13, God declares, "there is none who can deliver from my hand."[293] If no one can take another person out of God's hand, then even in those cases in which an individual is killed at the very earliest point of his temporal existence, that individual need not be lost to God.

When the implications of these biblical assertions are combined, it results in the following conclusions: (1) every person has free will; (2) at least part of this free will consists of a choice between placing faith in God or not placing faith in God; and (3) individuals can make this fundamental faith-based decision from the very inception of their existence. The first and second items in this three-part list were discussed earlier in this book, so the focus in the remaining pages of this chapter will be on the final item.

Earlier in this chapter, the key assumptions that underlie the "determinist" philosophy were identified and briefly explored. To review, determinists like Dr. Sapolsky assume that man is solely a material being, and further assume that all matter adheres to immutable rules of physics. Taken together, these two assumptions lead strict determinists to the conclusion that human decision-making is entirely predetermined. Experience, however, refutes this conclusion. The question therefore arises, if it is true that all matter follows immutable rules of physics, and if it is also true that man possesses genuine free will, is it not sensible to conclude that man is something more than just a material being?

Christianity asserts just this. It asserts that man's being consists of the unification of a physical body and an immaterial soul. The seat of man's free will is his soul. The mind and body implement the will of the soul to the extent that a person's finite mental and physical capacities permit him to do so at any given stage of life.

The will of the soul can be directed toward any number of different ends, but with respect to the question of salvation, the disposition of the soul can take one of only two forms. On the one hand, it can adopt a position of openness to the Source of life and love, even if this level of openness is exceedingly small. By necessity, this entails placing faith in God. Alternatively, it can choose to be faithless, which is a self-isolating choice.

At every point in its existence, the soul places itself in one or the other of these two camps. There is no in-between; there is no agnosticism of the soul. Because God's existence cannot be definitely proven or disproven as a matter of logic, an individual may refer to himself as "agnostic" when describing the state of his reasoning on the question of God's existence. In his soul, however, he either has at least a tiny seed of faith in God or he does not.

Said another way, at the deepest level of being, man is a faith-based creature. The essence of what he is as a being either consists of placing ultimate faith in himself, or it consists in some manner of reaching out in faith beyond himself toward God, even if only to a miniscule degree. There is never a point in man's existence when he is situated in some sort of "perfect middle" that is suspended in between faith and non-faith in God. There is no such middle position; the soul is always situated on one side or the other. The side a person chooses determines what he is at the most fundamental level of being: he is either a being who can enter into a loving relationship with the Source of love itself, or he is not.

The claim that individuals can make this key choice from the inception of their existence is perhaps the most difficult concept in this book to grasp because it requires a person to understand, however faintly, the practical operation of eternal existence. The reason a person must possess at least a faint understanding of the practical operation of eternal existence is because the soul itself is eternal.

As this book's previous discussions of timelessness have explained, the word "eternal" should be understood to refer to that which supersedes time. Consequently, the very assertion that the soul is "eternal" means that it supersedes time. If the soul supersedes time, and if the soul is the seat of man's faith-based decision-making concerning God, then by its very nature, the soul does not require time to make its fundamental decision for or against God.

This assertion is supported not only by Deuteronomy 32:39 and Isaiah 43:13 (the last biblical passages cited above), but also by John 8:44. In this verse, Christ states that the most powerful of the fallen angels was a murderer "from the beginning." It is evident that Jesus is not claiming that God purposefully created this angel to be evil, because Jesus also states in this passage that this angel is "the father of lies," not God.[294] If God is not the "father" of this angel's evil, it can only mean that this angel made a *choice* to adopt evil. This interpretation is confirmed by Isaiah 14:12–14, which describes the self-centered choice of this angel to try to occupy a position above God.[295]

The phrase "from the beginning" expresses that this choice was made from a state of timelessness—that is, from a state of existence superseding time. In such a state, every choice is made "from the beginning" because this state is not a linear, time-based form of existence. If Christ had instead been referring to a time-based state of existence in John 8:44, his statements in this passage would be self-contradicting. After all, a created being whose entire existence is linear cannot simultaneously be evil "from the beginning" and be the "father" of his own evil. The only way these two assertions can be reconciled with one another is if Christ is describing a choice that was freely made by a supratemporal being.

The choice whether to place faith in God is the free-willed decision that defines what each person is at his deepest level of being. Each person is the "father" of his own choice in this respect. This choice, like the one described in John 8:44, can be made without regard to time because it is a choice that is made by the supratemporal soul. To establish that this is not the case, one would have to know exactly how and why individuals make the choice to believe or disbelieve.

What was it, for example, that caused Robert Sapolsky at the age of fourteen to wake up in the dead of night and declare that there is no God? Clearly, he did not reason his way to this conclusion because he was asleep right up to the moment that he announced it to himself. A more sensible explanation of how he made his way to this conclusion is that it was an act of the will; it was what he *wanted* to believe, and therefore what he *chose* to believe, from the inmost level of his being—his soul.[296]

Of course, this cannot be established with absolute certainty. There are simply too many ambiguities involved to prove with certitude how or why a person makes the choice whether to believe or disbelieve. Some deny that any such ambiguity exists, insisting that faith is nothing more than a product of a person's upbringing and environment. But this claim ignores the many examples of people who arrive at devout faith after being raised in a godless environment, as well as people who become committed atheists after spending their childhood within a community of strong believers.

The use of these examples should in no way be construed as a claim that a person's upbringing cannot impact his ultimate choice of whether to believe. On the contrary, the knowledge and experience that people accumulate during the course of their temporal lives typically play an extremely important role in their decision whether to believe, perhaps even a decisive role. But the soul should not be conflated with the mind; the soul is something distinct from a person's accumulated temporal knowledge and experience.

As such, time is ultimately not necessary for the soul to make its choice whether to believe. Again, if faith is a choice that is made by the soul, and if the soul is timeless, then man's faith-based decision-making need not be contingent on time; it need only be contingent on existence. Said differently, a soul's existence as a timeless living entity is the only precondition necessary for it to choose faith or faithlessness.

Because the decision whether to place faith in God is *the* choice that defines whether a person enters into an eternal loving relationship with God, and because this choice is made by the eternal soul, a temporal existence of any duration whatsoever is, in the final analysis, sufficient for the soul to make its choice. If a temporal existence of any duration at all is sufficient for the soul to decide whether to place faith in God, it follows that there is no circumstance in the diversity of human experience that establishes that something more than faith is required of a person for salvation. Faith alone is sufficient.

CONCLUSION

If there is no God, then everything that exists is here through some incredible series of happenstance events. If everything in existence is here as the result of pure happenstance, originating from a principal cause that itself occurred for no explicable reason, then nothing has any intrinsic meaning, value, or purpose. It simply is.[297] By definition, there is no inherent purpose or meaning to life that is here arbitrarily.

But if man is nothing more than the product of purposeless, chance events, why is it that in every society on Earth, in every generation, people find themselves searching for the "purpose" and "meaning" of life instead of focusing their attention solely on worldly issues? Why, unlike every other creature in this world, is man religious?[298]

Man's contemplation of these types of questions leads him to consider the possibility that everything is not here arbitrarily.[299] God could be the cause of everything that exists,[300] but why would God create man?[301] Christianity's answer is that God created man for the purpose of entering into an eternal loving union with him.[302] The *Catechism* states that this is "the definitive, superabundant answer to the questions that man asks himself about the meaning and purpose of his life."[303] But if God is omnipotent and omnibenevolent, and if God made man for the purpose of entering into an eternal loving union with him, why do pain, suffering, and death exist?

On the surface, this question seems unanswerable. Indeed, the problem of pain is unsolvable when one approaches it unmindful of the fact that love cannot occur without the presence of certain prerequisites. When unawareness of this fact is combined with a dismissive attitude regarding the consequences of sin, or a superficial understanding of God's nature and character, the result is always the same—the conclusion that God is either not powerful enough or loving enough to prevent pain, which means that God must not exist.

People arrive at this same conclusion whenever they attempt to find reasons to justify particular instances of suffering. Any such attempt is a hopeless enterprise, a point made in numerous biblical discourses on suffering.[304] Stories like the one given in Job make it clear that the punishment for wrongdoing is not meted out in a tit-for-tat manner, with each sin earning a countervailing punishment in the form of some specific experience of pain or suffering.

Instead, the punishment for sin is the fall to a sinful state of existence. The fall to such a state of existence is not something that affects only one or two facets of man's being. Instead, sin is all-consuming; it reduces man's entire being to an enfeebled, corrupted version of its original state. Sin, moreover, disorders and perverts everything placed under man's realm of authority, including the very foundation of the material order itself.

One of the consequences of living in a fallen state and realm of existence is susceptibility to pain. Said another way, pain and suffering are merely symptoms of the underlying problem with man. Sin is the fundamental problem with man, a point Jesus made powerfully during his interaction with the paralytic in Mark 2:1–12. Joseph Ratzinger considers "this whole scene to be of key significance for the question of Jesus' mission," writing:

Jesus himself poignantly raised the question as to where the priority lies in man's need for redemption on the occasion when the four men, who could not carry the paralytic through the door because of the crowd, let him down from the roof and laid him at Jesus' feet. The sick man's very existence was a plea, an urgent appeal for salvation, to which Jesus responded in a way that was quite contrary to the expectation of the bearers and of the sick man himself, saying: "My son, your sins are forgiven". This was the last thing anyone was expecting. This was the last thing they were concerned about. The paralytic needed to be able to walk, not to be delivered from his sins...the sick man and those around him were disappointed, because Jesus had apparently overlooked the man's real need.[305]

Of course, Jesus had overlooked nothing. Ratzinger continues: "The priority of forgiveness for sins as the foundation of all true healing is clearly maintained. Man is a relational being. And if his first, fundamental relationship is disturbed—his relationship with God—then nothing else can be truly in order. There is where the priority lies in Jesus' message and ministry: before all else, he wants to point man toward the essence of his malady, and to show him—if you are not healed *there*, then however many good things you find, you are not truly healed."[306]

According to both Genesis and Jesus, man's sin is the root cause of all pain, suffering, and death in the world. Man enters the world in a sinful state of being because of the actions of Adam and Eve, who changed the underlying basis of their existence by committing sin when they existed in a supratemporal state of being. Made in the "likeness" of the timeless, omnipotent God, the changes wrought by the first humans' sin are holistic in nature and scope.[307] These changes were so expansive that they caused all forms of life placed under man's "dominion"—at all points across the full continuum of existence—to mirror the first humans' willful self-centeredness and deliberate indifference toward God at the moment of their fall from timelessness.[308] As evolution makes readily apparent, when every form of life engages in self-furthering action while remaining indifferent or otherwise blind to the effects of such self-centeredness on other life forms, universal suffering and death are the inevitable result.[309]

This understanding of the underlying cause of the forces that propel evolution provides a clearer picture of the scope of the fall. It was an event of such enormity that it simultaneously reordered *everything* in physical creation, even the material order itself, changing it from a timeless state of being to one that is time-based. When the scale of the fall is seen from this perspective, the reasonableness of identifying original sin as the ultimate source of all suffering and death in the natural world should be apparent.

Following the fall, God allowed the progeny of Adam and Eve to suffer the consequences of original sin for the sake of allowing humanity, as a body,[310] the opportunity to continue to experience love. More precisely, humanity exists only because God prioritized love before justice when mankind committed the first act of sin, and he continued to prioritize love before justice with each subsequent act of sin. If God had instead placed justice before love when Adam and Eve first committed sin, mankind would have been put to an end long ago.

Obviously, it would have been senseless if God had made this latter decision. There is no reason an omniscient God would bother to create life if he knew from the outset that his creatures would sin, and if he knew further that he would immediately impose the full, fair penalty of sin on them as soon as they went astray. What would be the point of creating them in the first place?

If God is rational, then creation must have an intelligible purpose. Consider some of the possible purposes God could pursue. Would an all-wise God create just because he could? Is there any wisdom in such a decision? Would an omnipotent God create beings as feeble as fallen man for the primary purpose of having man worship God? Would this not show that God, far from being all-powerful, instead suffers from a staggering lack of self-esteem? Would an omniscient God create sentient beings for the sake of seeing what they would do with their free will? Can there be anything more pointless? Would an omnibenevolent God allow creation to descend into the violent, debauched state that it has become without having some greater objective in mind?

If God would not have allowed his creation to descend to such a state without some greater purpose in mind, what is this purpose? What objective could possibly be worth the suffering that man and lesser creatures endure in this world? There is only one conceivable answer: love. If God exists, and if God is omnipotent, omnibenevolent, and omniscient, then love is the only plausible explanation for man's existence.

Indeed, love is the only logical reason for God to create anything at all. No other purpose or goal is worth pursuing because no other objective could possibly hold any value to an omnipotent being. For an omnipotent being, any goal other than love would be an absurdity. One merely has to consider the various other goals God could pursue to see the sheer pointlessness of them all. Aside from love, there is simply no reason for an omnipotent being to create.[311]

If love is the only intelligible creative objective, then it is only reasonable to conclude that God will act to bring about the highest possible form of this objective. As the German polymath Gottfried

Wilhelm Leibniz argued, out of an infinite number of possible creative ends, logic demands that an all-knowing, all-powerful being will choose the greatest end that can be brought to fruition; he will create "the best of all possible worlds."[312] The most grandiose conceivable creative objective is specified in Revelation 7:9, which describes "a great multitude" of beings so vast that "no man could number" them,[313] becoming one body with God in an eternal loving union.[314]

For creatures to be so much like God that they are able to join to him in a timeless loving unity of being, they would need to be vested with attributes like those of God himself. First and foremost, they would need to possess the ability to love. But to be able to love at the breadth and degree that God loves, they would need to be beings with the capacity to exercise truly godlike dominion over lesser creatures; they would need to have the ability to create other living beings like themselves through acts of love; and they would need to wield power so immense that they could determine for themselves the basis of their own nature, down to the most elemental, structural level of being. These are the traits of man described in Genesis 1–3.

If God decides to create man for the sake of entering into a reciprocal loving relationship with him, negative consequences will inevitably ensue if man decides to prioritize a selfish end over this loving relationship. Justice dictates that the negative consequences of such decision-making be imposed on the individuals who undermined love through their prioritization of a self-centered objective. But if these consequences are imposed on man in their entirety as soon as he commits his first wrongful act, love is extinguished along with man. If love is extinguished, the whole purpose of creation is defeated.

Hence the central question in God's creative plan emerges: is it wiser to prevent the first humans from unjustly imposing the costs of their sin on others, which can only be accomplished by either annihilating them or dispossessing them of the powers that are necessary for them to experience love at the same range and degree as God, or is love so valuable that it is worth allowing Adam and Eve to impose sin and its penalty on both their offspring and the lesser creatures placed under their dominion, even though neither of these groups has done anything to warrant such a fate?[315]

God's decision-making with respect to this question is entirely logical and perfectly consistent with his all-loving, all-just, and all-wise nature. But to understand why this is the case, one must first understand that the ultimate objective of God's creative plan is for man and God to become a loving unity with one another.[316] The question for us is whether we can bring ourselves to have faith that God's plan for man is truly as resplendent as the Bible asserts. Our experience of living in a sinful, fallen condition—our experience of suffering—can be a powerful obstacle to such belief.

The suffering we endure as a result of the wrongful actions of others is not an easy burden to bear, nor is it a burden we must bear infrequently. All throughout life we find ourselves suffering because of the sins of others. In so doing, we emulate Christ's suffering for love. Just as Christ suffered the injustice of our sin for the sake of allowing us the opportunity to enter into a full and loving relationship with God following our earthly lives, we suffer the injustices imposed on us by the misdeeds of others for the sake of allowing them, and us, the continued opportunity to experience love in this life, as well as the opportunity to expand the overall domain of love for all eternity.

Man's experience of pain is full of the most profound meaning when one realizes that we suffer for the sake of love. When the problem of pain is approached with this realization, we can understand how we become more like Christ—and therefore more like the Triune God—with each new unfair experience of suffering we endure. Though this does not make our experience of pain less difficult, it transforms our suffering into a privileged burden.

The weight of this burden is, at times, heavy enough to make even the most devout believers question God's wisdom in valuing love to such a high degree. In these moments, our faith in God is strained, and in some cases, it is strained right up to its breaking point. As our faith in God is pushed to its outermost limit by the "LORD of hosts, who test[s] the righteous,"[317] it grows, expanding beyond our experience of pain, beyond fear, beyond even death itself. As our faith overcomes every obstacle and boundary, we grow more and more into an image of Christ, who overcame the greatest of all obstacles to love on the basis of his unyielding faith in God the Father.

According to Habakkuk 1:13, God the Father is "too pure to look upon wickedness."[318] Because of this, he turned away when the Son of man assumed culpability for humanity's evil, and "did not spare his own Son but gave him up for us all."[319] In Christ's position as the bearer of the sins of all mankind,[320] he experienced the same sense of forsakenness from God the Father that we experience in our own lives. This becomes apparent at the moment when, in a reference to his fulfillment of the Suffering Servant prophesy in Psalm 22 while hanging on the cross, Christ loudly proclaims that he has been "forsaken" by God the Father.[321] In the face of this experience of separation from the Father, Christ's suffering for love had to be endured on the basis of faith.

For those who question why Christ's sacrifice had to be performed on the basis of faith, the answer is straightforward: love is not possible without faith, and the greater the obstacle faith must overcome, the more powerful is the love that results. Sin is the greatest of all obstacles to love. Sin represents the extreme, polar opposite of love, and for this reason it exists at the furthest-most distance from God, an infinite distance.[322] Only God, an infinite being, could bridge such a distance. This bridge is accomplished by and through Jesus Christ, the begotten Son of God and the begotten Son of man—the unification of the Creator and the created in one being, fully God and fully man. As Christ took the sins of mankind upon himself, substituting himself for us, he willingly placed himself at an immeasurable distance from God the Father.

This place of immeasurable distance has a name: Calvary. There, staked to a wooden cross by the depraved creatures he was sacrificing himself to save,[323] only faith could traverse the limitless distance between the Son of sinful man and God the Father. Christ's faith, moreover, was and is so perfect that it meets death, then supersedes it, without being diminished in the slightest degree.[324]

In this spanning of the infinite distance, this marvel of love,[325] God freely and lovingly gave to fallen man that which mankind cannot provide for himself. Two lovers may desire to have a love so perfect that it will not be diminished in the slightest degree though they are separated from one another on opposite ends of the world. They may desire to make their love so total, so complete, that they overcome the vast distance between them in order to enter fully and wholly into one another, bonding into one being.[326]

We may desire to experience a love like this—love in its truest, fullest form—but while we remain mired in a sinful state of existence, we cannot know such love. Our beings, consumed as they are with self-centeredness and indifference toward others, must die before we can experience love of this degree. But to experience love of this degree, we, like Christ at the time of his sacrifice for our sin, must have faith in God in spite of our experience of suffering and separation from him, for it is only through faith that can we enter into a relationship in which we become one with God in love.

Nothing short of this perfect, divine love will fill the void within man. This is why we are told to love God with all our heart, mind, and soul,[327] because it is only by doing so that we can fulfill the purpose of our creation and thereby attain salvation. This salvation, though, can only be achieved through faith. After all, if salvation consists of entering into a loving union with God, and if faith is a precondition of love, including love between us and God, then our salvation is ultimately a product of our faith.

Just as love is not possible without faith, love between two individuals cannot be greater than the faith they are each willing to place in one another. It should go without saying that God does not want us to experience a tepid, mediocre love with him. God wants us to experience an extreme love with him, and extreme love is only possible when both parties have extreme faith in one another. For this reason, we should expect our faith to be stretched and pulled to its outermost limit during the course of our temporal lives. We should expect, moreover, the process of growing our faith to be afflicting.[328]

As the case of Job demonstrates, God will allow those with the greatest faith to face the most inscrutable hardships in order that they may have the opportunity to exercise even greater faith.[329] When difficult and seemingly inexplicable tests of our faith occur, we should remember that it is the inexplicableness of the challenges to our belief in God that enables us to exercise faith in the first place. If we could provide a comprehensive and conclusive answer to every challenge that is given to our belief, we would have no ability to exercise faith, and therefore no ability to experience love with God. Faith is the continuance of belief in the face of the uncertain and the unknown.

Many individuals think it foolhardy to believe in God in the absence of proof. Some even regard such belief with outright contempt, viewing it as a sign of ineptitude or weakness. Their belief is that it is more reasonable to focus our energies exclusively on the here and now, in spite of the fact that death ultimately renders all of our temporal-focused efforts meaningless.[330] For such people, faith in God is not understood as a sensible commitment undertaken by thoughtful people fighting to live up to the exacting requirements of love in the face of temptations to surrender to egocentric desires.[331] Instead, faith is seen as a practice undertaken only by people who are either too childlike[332] to recognize that God does not exist, or too afraid to accept that this life is the only one there is. The courage required to selflessly submit to God in faith is not seen as a form of bravery. Instead, this essential sacrifice for the sake of love is viewed with disgust, as a frailty and a stupidity.

It is probably inevitable that those with the greatest faith in God will be ridiculed by those who focus their attention exclusively on worldly objectives. In many cases, we find ourselves placing faith in temporal ends because we convince ourselves that we will find a measure of happiness, or at least a degree of protection from certain kinds of suffering, if we can only become wealthy, successful, respected. John Henry Cardinal Newman summarized this attitude toward wealth and fame as follows: "Wealth is that to which the multitude of men pay an instinctive homage. They measure happiness by wealth; and by wealth they measure respectability... It is a homage resulting from a profound faith...that with wealth he may do all things. Wealth is one idol of the day and notoriety is a second... Notoriety, or the making of noise in the world—it may be called 'newspaper fame'—has come to be considered a great good in itself, and a ground of veneration."[333]

Of course, anyone who carefully and soberly considers the reality of the human condition must eventually conclude that such finite ends do not guarantee happiness or provide assurance that a person will be spared from terrible experiences of suffering, pain, and loss. On the contrary, people are apt to grow shrewd and shallow when they place great levels of faith in the security and happiness supposedly provided by material wealth, power, fame, or social status. When such misplaced faith grows strong enough, people will willingly sacrifice anything and anyone for it.[334]

Love is the casualty of placing faith in the wrong ends. As long as our selfish desires stand between us and the love we are meant to experience with God and one another, there is no hope for true happiness. Even if our selfish aspirations propel us to the most towering heights of influence, wealth, and prestige, these so-called "accomplishments" never result in lasting happiness.[335] The *Catechism* asserts, "True happiness is not found in riches or well-being, in human fame or power, or in any human achievement—however beneficial it may be—such as science, technology, and art, or indeed in any creature, but in God alone, the source of every good and of all love."[336]

"God alone satisfies."[337] This is why, whenever the object of a person's selfish desires is obtained, there always remains a sense that something is still amiss, a feeling that some sort of need has not yet been met. According to the *Catechism*, "This desire is of divine origin: God has placed it in the human heart in order to draw man to the One who alone can fulfill it."[338]

The longing for something greater than that which can be provided by the attainment of self-centered ends is an inescapable reality of the human condition. But even when this reality of our existence becomes apparent, even when our realization of it leads us to perceive that we are being called to abandon our hopeless faith in our endless selfish desires,[339] many still refuse to redirect their faith toward God because they are afraid of being deceived into believing something that may not be true.

Perhaps more than anything else it is fear of deception that prevents people from turning to God in faith. As to this final, most critical issue, Søren Kierkegaard had the following to say:

> Indeed, one can be deceived in many ways; one can be deceived in believing what is untrue, but on the other hand, one is also deceived in not believing what is true; one can be deceived by appearances, but one can also be deceived by the superficiality of shrewdness, by the flattering conceit which is absolutely certain that it cannot be deceived. Which deception is more dangerous?...
>
> To cheat oneself out of love is the most terrible deception; it is an eternal loss for which there is no reparation...
>
> In the temporal world a man may succeed in getting along without love; he may succeed in slipping through life without discovering the self-deception; he may have the terrible success, in his conceit, of becoming proud of it; but in eternity he cannot dispense with love and cannot escape discovering that he has lost everything.[340]

REFERENCES

1   John W. Loftus, *Why I Became an Atheist: A Former Preacher Rejects Christianity* (Amherst, NY: Prometheus Books, 2008), 228.

2   Loftus, *Why I Became an Atheist*, 230. Loftus cites numerous reasons for his abandonment of Christianity, but in Chapter 12, he identifies the problem of evil as the most intellectually powerful argument against the Christian faith, declaring that it is "as close to an empirical refutation of Christianity as is possible."

3   Loftus, *Why I Became an Atheist*, 235.

4   Augustine of Hippo, *City of God*, trans. Henry Bettenson (427; repr., London: Penguin, 2003), 454.

5   Later, it will become clear that evil precedes pain and that evil is, in fact, the underlying cause of all pain and suffering.

6   Bart D. Ehrman, *God's Problem: How the Bible Fails to Answer Our Most Important Question—Why We Suffer* (New York: HarperCollins, 2008), 12.

7   John Hick, *Evil and the God of Love*, rev. ed. (1977; repr., New York: Palgrave Macmillan, 2010), 256–59.

8   John 16:12 states that God does not provide man with information about divine matters before man is in a position to bear it. As will become apparent in subsequent chapters, the solution to the problem of evil cannot be truly understood without first having a general understanding of the well-established findings of natural science. Without the hard-won discoveries of physicists, astronomers, geologists, and evolutionary biologists, mankind would not comprehend the foundational role of time in physics, the vast size of the universe, the immense age of the Earth, or the depraved mechanisms

that propel the development of life in the physical realm. All these scientific findings are essential for mankind to understand the staggering scope and scale of the fall. In the absence of this understanding, man is left with a diminished appreciation of his stature as a being, which in turn prevents him from comprehending the solution to the problem of evil.

9   A. M. Weisberger, *Suffering Belief: Evil and the Anglo-American Defense of Theism* (New York: Peter Lang, 1999), 102.

10   *Catechism of the Catholic Church* (New York: Doubleday, 1994), 309.

11   Because this book aligns most closely with Catholic doctrine, Catholic translations of the Bible are utilized. The Catholic translations that are referenced are the Revised Standard Version, Second Catholic Edition (RSV-2CE); the New Revised Standard Version, Catholic Edition (NRSV-CE); and the New American Bible, Revised Edition (NABRE).

12   Regarding the doctrinal value of the *Catechism*, Pope John Paul II wrote, "The *Catechism of the Catholic Church*, which I approved June 25th last and the publication of which I today order by virtue of my Apostolic Authority, is a statement of the Church's faith and of catholic doctrine, attested to or illuminated by Sacred Scripture, the Apostolic Tradition, and the Church's Magisterium. I declare it to be a sure norm for teaching the faith and thus a valid and legitimate instrument for ecclesial communion." *Catechism of the Catholic Church, Apostolic Constitution, Fidei Depositum*, October 11, 1992.

13   In David Hume's *Dialogues Concerning Natural Religion*, the character Philo provides one of the most oft-quoted descriptions of the Epicurean problem: "Is he [God] willing to prevent evil, but not able? Then he is impotent. Is he able, but not willing? Then he is malevolent. Is he both able and willing? Whence then is evil?" *Dialogues Concerning Natural Religion*, 2nd ed. (1779; repr., Indianapolis, IN: Hackett Publishing, 1988), 63.

14   Each of these four assertions coincides with descriptions of God's attributes found in the Bible:

(1)   God is all-powerful: Genesis 18:14, Psalm 62:11, First Chronicles 29:11, Jeremiah 32:27, and Matthew 19:26.

(2)   God is all-loving: First John 4:8 and 16.

(3)   God is all-just: Genesis 18:25, Isaiah 30:18, Deuteronomy 32:4, Psalm 18:30, Daniel 4:37, Second Chronicles 19:7, and First John 1:5.

(4)   God is all-knowing/all-wise: First Chronicles 28:9, Job 37:16, Psalm 139:1–4, and Isaiah 42:9.

15   (NRSV-CE) Further biblical support for the assertion that God ranks love over all other considerations can be found in Mark 12:28–34, Luke 10:25–28, and First Corinthians 13:13–21.

16   "There does not fall under the scope of God's omnipotence anything that implies a contradiction." Saint Thomas Aquinas, *Summa Theologica*, Complete American Edition (1485; repr., Claremont, CA: Coyote Canyon Press, 2018), 86.

17   When God creates a being with an eternal soul, like man, it represents a permanent transfer of power.

18   The act of vesting Adam with a portion of God's power is described in Genesis 2:7, when God breathed into Adam's nostrils "the breath of life." (RSV-2CE)

19   "God has not willed to reserve to himself all exercise of power. He entrusts to every creature the functions it is capable of performing, according to the capacities of its own nature." *Catechism of the Catholic Church*, 1884.

20   Simone Weil, "Forms of the Implicit Love of God," in *Waiting for God*, trans. Emma Craufurd (1951; repr., New York: Harper Perennial Modern Classics, 2009), 89.

21   The opening words of the *Catechism of the Catholic Church* assert that the purpose of man's life is "To Know and Love God."

22   The "Great Commandment" appears in the New Testament in Matthew 22:34–40, Mark 12:28–34, and Luke 10:25–28. It is derived from Deuteronomy 6:5 and Leviticus 19:18 in the Old Testament.

23   Conrad Hackett and David McClendon, "Christians Remain World's Largest Religious Group, but They Are Declining in Europe," Pew Research Center, April 5, 2017, https://www.pewresearch.org/

fact-tank/2017/04/05/christians-remain-worlds-largest-religious-group-but-they-are-declining-in-europe/.

24   (RSV-2CE)

25   Ed Diener and Martin E. P. Seligman, "Very Happy People," *Psychological Science* 13, no. 1 (2002): 81–84.

26   Julia M. Rohrer, David Richter, Martin Brümmer, Gert G. Wagner, and Stefan C. Schmukle, "Successfully Striving for Happiness: Socially Engaged Pursuits Predict Increases in Life Satisfaction," *Psychological Science* 29, no. 8 (2018): 1291–98.

27   Neal Krause, Gail Ironson, and Peter Hill, "Religious Involvement and Happiness: Assessing the Mediating Role of Compassion and Helping Others," *The Journal of Social Psychology* 158, no. 2 (2018): 256–70.

28   Alex J. Bishop, P. Martin, and L. Poon, "Happiness and Congruence in Older Adulthood: A Structural Model of Life Satisfaction," *Aging & Mental Health* 10, no. 5 (2006): 445–53; Robert J. Waldinger and Marc S. Schulz, "What's Love Got To Do With It?: Social Functioning, Perceived Health, and Daily Happiness in Married Octogenarians," *Psychology and Aging* 25, no. 2 (2010): 422–31.

29   Viviana Amati, Silvia Meggiolaro, Giulia Rivellini, and Susanna Zaccarin, "Social Relation and Life Satisfaction: The Role of Friends," *Genus* 74, no. 1 (2018): 7. Quoted language taken from the abstract.

30   Erin Y. Cornwell, and Linda J. Waite, "Social Disconnectedness, Perceived Isolation, and Health among Older Adults," *Journal of Health and Social Behavior* 50, no. 1 (2009): 31–48; John T. Cacioppo, Mary Elizabeth Hughes, Lousie C. Hawkley, and Ronald A. Thisted, "Loneliness as a Specific Risk Factor for Depressive Symptoms: Cross-Sectional and Longitudinal Analyses," *Psychology and Aging* 21, no. 1 (2006): 140–51.

31   Keramet Reiter, Joseph Ventura, David Lovell, Dallas Augustine, Melissa Barragan, Thomas Blair, Kelsie Chesnut, Pasha Dashtgard, Gabriela Gonzolez, Natalie Pifer, and Justin Strong, "Psychological Distress in Solitary Confinement: Symptoms, Severity, and Prevalence

in the United States, 2017–2018," *American Journal of Public Health* 110, no. 1 (2020): S56–S62.

32   One study found that unhappiness is greater in societies suffering from high levels of corruption and other forms of pervasive self-centeredness that serve to undermine friendship at a societal scale. Cf. Ruut Veenhoven, "Greater Happiness for a Greater Number: Is that possible and desirable?" *Journal of Happiness Studies* 11, no. 5 (2010): 605–29. The positive effects of social interaction on human health have been established not only in the field of psychology but have also been discovered by researchers in the fields of epidemiology, biology, and medicine. Cf. T. E. Seeman, "Social Ties and Health: The Benefits of Social Integration," *Annals of Epidemiology* 6, no. 5 (1996): 442–51; John T. Cacioppo and Louise C. Hawkley, "Social Isolation and Health, with an Emphasis on Underlying Mechanisms," *Perspectives in Biology and Medicine* 46, no. 3 (2003): S39–S52; Elliot M. Friedman, Mary S. Hayney, Gayle D. Love, Heather L. Urry, Melissa A. Rosenkranz, Richard J. Davidson, Burton H. Singer, and Carol D. Ryff, "Social Relationships, Sleep Quality, and Interleukin-6 in Aging Women," *Proceedings of the National Academy of Sciences of the United States of America* 102, no. 51 (2005): 18757–62.

33   Christopher P. Niemiec, Richard M. Ryan, and Edward L. Deci, "The Path Taken: Consequences of Attaining Intrinsic and Extrinsic Aspirations in Post-College Life," *Journal of Research in Personality* 43, no. 3 (2009): 291–306.

34   Daniel Kahneman and Angus Deaton, "High Income Improves Evaluation of Life but Not Emotional Well-Being," *Proceedings of the National Academy of Sciences of the United States of America* 107, no. 38 (2010): 16489–93.

35   One study discovered significant differences in the physiologic effects stemming from altruistic pleasures versus those stemming from hedonistic pleasures. This study found that self-centered pleasures made cells in the immune system act like they were under stress, whereas pleasures stemming from helping others caused the opposite response. Barbara L. Fredrickson, Karen M. Grewen, Kimberly A. Coffey, Sara B. Algoe, Ann M. Firestine, Jesusa M. G. Arevalo, Jeffrey Ma, and Steven W. Cole, "A Functional Genomic

Perspective on Human Well-Being," *Proceedings of the National Academy of Sciences of the United States of America* 110, no. 33 (2013): 13684–89.

36   Danny G. Blanchflower and Andrew J. Oswald, "Money, Sex and Happiness: An Empirical Study," *The Scandinavian Journal of Economics* 106, no. 3 (2004): 393–415.

37   Kira S. Birditt and Toni C. Antonucci, "Relationship quality profiles and well-being among married adults," *Journal of Family Psychology* 21, no. 4 (2007): 595–604. From the abstract: "Among people with best friends, having at least 2 high quality relations, not necessarily with a spouse, is associated with greater well-being."

38   Harvard Medical School, "Study of Adult Development," Harvard Second Generation Study, 2015, https://www.adultdevelopmentstudy.org/grantandglueckstudy.

39   Harvard Medical School, "Study of Adult Development."

40   John F. Kennedy

41   Melanie Curtin, "This 75-Year Harvard Study Found the 1 Secret to Leading a Fulfilling Life," *Inc.*, February 2017, https://www.inc.com/melanie-curtin/want-a-life-of-fulfillment-a-75-year-harvard-study-says-to-prioritize-this-one-t.html.

42   Joshua Wolf Shenk, "What Makes Us Happy?: Is There a Formula—Some Mix of Love, Work, and Psychological Adaptation—for a Good Life?" *The Atlantic*, June 2009, https://www.theatlantic.com/magazine/archive/2009/06/what-makes-us-happy/307439/.

43   George Vaillant, *Triumphs of Experience: The Men of the Harvard Grant Study* (Cambridge, MA: The Belknap Press, 2012). Vaillant on the importance of love:

- "I stand by my rash assertion to *The Atlantic* that relationships (that is, the capacity for loving attachment) is what matters most in life" (191–92).

- "So what do the seventy-five years of the Grant Study have to teach us about marriage, intimacy, and mental health? For one thing, they make clear that Lewellen Howland was right—the

important thing is that 'loving people for a long time is good'"
(221).

- "[T]he most important contributor to joy and success in adult
life is love" (370).

44   Scott Stossel, "What Makes Us Happy, Revisited: A New Look
at the famous Harvard Study of What Makes People Thrive,"
The Atlantic, May 2013, https://www.theatlantic.com/magazine/
archive/2013/05/thanks-mom/309287/.

45   Aristotle, *The Nicomachean Ethics*, trans. David Ross (New York:
Oxford University Press, 2009), 142.

46   (RSV-2CE)

47   "There are friends who pretend to be friends, but there is a
friend who sticks closer than a brother." (RSV-2CE)

48   (RSV-2CE)

49   "Greater love has no man than this, that a man lay down his life
for his friends." (RSV-2CE)

50   John 1:1–14 asserts that the "Word became flesh" in the form
of Jesus Christ, who commanded man to love God and one another.
(NRSV-CE) However, Christ did not appear in a manner or form
that would usurp man's ability to make a truly free choice whether to
enter into a loving relationship with God. "Christ invited people to
faith and conversion, but never coerced them." *Catechism of the Catholic
Church*, 160.

51   (RSV-2CE)

52   Galatians 5:14: "For the whole law is fulfilled in one word, 'You
shall love your neighbor as yourself.'" (RSV-2CE); James 2:8: "If you
really fulfil the royal law, according to Scripture, 'You shall love your
neighbor as yourself,' you do well." (RSV-2CE)

53   *Catechism of the Catholic Church*, 1957.

54   René Descartes, *Principles of Philosophy*. (1644; repr., Radford, VA:
Wilder Publications, 2008), Part I.

55   Descartes, *Principles of Philosophy*, 21.

56   This essential limitation of human reasoning appears to have been recognized by thinkers at least as far back as Aristotle. In section 1006a of *Metaphysics*, Aristotle declares, "It is impossible that there should be a demonstration of absolutely everything; there would be an infinite regress, so that there would still be no demonstration." An infinite regress occurs whenever an attempt is made to prove that which is assumed in an argument. Any attempt to demonstrate the soundness of a starting presupposition in an argument will require a second argument to be constructed that relies upon another assumed premise, which itself must be proven by relying on yet another assumption, and on and on, ad infinitum.

57   Man cannot ascertain the validity of even the simplest argument without presupposing his reasoning abilities are a reliable tool for examining reality and acquiring knowledge. Placing faith in one's reasoning abilities is a prerequisite for judging the soundness of any reason-based argument. Since man in his present state of existence cannot know with certainty whether his mind is the product of purposeful design or a long series of happenstance events, man has no wholly reliable basis to even place faith in his own reasoning abilities. Faith, therefore, underlies both nontheistic and theistic reasoning. No one can escape faith-based logic.

58   Paul Tillich, *Dynamics of Faith* (New York: HarperOne, 2009), 9.

59   As stated in Second Timothy 3:16, "All Scripture is inspired by God and profitable for teaching, for reproof, for correction, and for training in righteousness, that the man of God may be complete, equipped for every good work." (RSV-2CE) On this basis, quotes from Scripture are relied upon to provide the foundation for the most important arguments in Part II of this book.

60   "In this is love, not that we have loved God but that he loved us and sent his Son to be the expiation for our sins." (RSV-2CE)

61   Cf. Romans 5:12: "sin came into the world through one man and death through sin, and so death spread to all men because all men sinned." (RSV-2CE) *Catechism of the Catholic Church*, 602: "Man's sins, following on original sin, are punishable by death."

62   Tillich, *Dynamics of Faith*, 132–33.

63   This assertion is based on the author's personal observations and experiences while at war in Iraq, which served as the impetus for this book.

64   The forging of exceptionally close friendships in war is a well-known phenomenon and a recurring subject of literature and film. Cf. William Guarnere, Edward Heffron, and Robyn Post, *Brothers in Battle, Best of Friends: Two WWII Paratroopers from the Original Band of Brothers Tell Their Story* (Toronto, ON: Dutton Caliber, 2007).

65   Joseph Ratzinger (Pope Benedict XVI), *Eschatology: Death and Eternal Life* (Washington, DC: The Catholic University of America Press, 1988), 107.

66   Ratzinger, *Eschatology: Death and Eternal Life*, 106.

67   (RSV-2CE)

68   *Catechism of the Catholic Church*, 356.

69   *Catechism of the Catholic Church*, 340.

70   *Catechism of the Catholic Church*, 356.

71   *Catechism of the Catholic Church*, 356.

72   *Catechism of the Catholic Church*, 357.

73   *Catechism of the Catholic Church*, 238–56. Cf. Matthew 28:18–20, in which Christ instructs his disciples to baptize "in the name of the Father and of the Son and of the Holy Spirit." (RSV-2CE)

74   C. S. Lewis, *The Problem of Pain* (1940; repr., New York: HarperOne, 2001), 20.

75   (RSV-2CE) Cf. *Catechism of the Catholic Church*, 2331: "God is love and in himself he lives a mystery of personal loving communion."

76   "Disfigured by sin and death, man remains 'in the image of God,' in the image of the Son, but is deprived 'of the glory of God,' of his 'likeness.'" *Catechism of the Catholic Church*, 705. As a result, fallen man cannot exercise command over the material order in the same manner as God, nor can fallen man experience omnipresence in the same manner as God. (The relevance of these two points will become clear in subsequent chapters.)

77   Genesis 5:2 (RSV-2CE)

78   Genesis 2:24 (RSV-2CE)

79   *Catechism of the Catholic Church*, 383. Cf. *Catechism of the Catholic Church*, 2331: "God is love and in himself he lives a mystery of personal loving communion. Creating the human race in his own image... God inscribed in the humanity of man and woman the *vocation*, and thus the capacity and responsibility, *of love* and communion."

80   *Catechism of the Catholic Church*, 1878.

81   *Catechism of the Catholic Church*, 1604.

82   Matthew 22:36–40 (RSV-2CE)

83   "And the Lord God commanded the man, saying, 'You may freely eat of every tree of the garden; but of the tree of the knowledge of good and evil you shall not eat, for in the day that you eat of it you shall die.'" (RSV-2CE)

84   Cf. *Catechism of the Catholic Church*, 374–79.

85   (RSV-2CE) Cf. Romans 6:23: "For the wages of sin is death." (RSV-2CE)

86   "Evil" is synonymous with "sin." The *Catechism of the Catholic Church* provides the following definitions of sin:

- "Only in the knowledge of God's plan for man can we grasp that sin is an abuse of the freedom that God gives to created persons so that they are capable of loving him and loving one another." *Catechism of the Catholic Church*, 387.

- "Sin is...failure in genuine love for God and neighbor caused by a perverse attachment to certain goods." *Catechism of the Catholic Church*, 1849.

- "Sin sets itself against God's love for us and turns our hearts away from it... Sin is thus 'love of oneself even to contempt of God.'" *Catechism of the Catholic Church*, 1850.

87   Wisdom 2:23: "God created man for incorruption." (RSV-2CE) Wisdom 1:13: "God did not make death, and he does not delight in the death of the living." (RSV-2CE)

88   "Man, tempted by the devil, let his trust in his Creator die in his heart and, abusing his freedom, disobeyed God's command. This is what man's first sin consisted of. All subsequent sin would be disobedience toward God and lack of trust in his goodness. In that sin man *preferred* himself to God and by that very act scorned him. He chose himself over and against God." *Catechism of the Catholic Church*, 397–98.

89   This is a critical point, the significance of which will become clear in the ensuing chapters.

90   Romans 6:23: "For the wages of sin is death." (RSV-2CE)

91   *Catechism of the Catholic Church*, 390. Protestant doctrine on the fall cannot be summarized as succinctly as Catholic teaching on this subject, but the predominant view among Protestants is likewise that Genesis 3 describes an actual event. Cf. Norman L. Geisler and Ralph E. MacKenzie, *Roman Catholics and Evangelicals: Agreements and Differences* (Grand Rapids, MI: Baker, 1995), 53–65. "Catholics and evangelicals share a common view of the origin, nature, and fall of human beings. Both believe God is the creator, human beings are made in his image and likeness, and human beings are immortal" (53). Cf. John Adam Moehler, trans. James Burton Robertson, *Symbolism or Exposition on the Doctrinal Differences Between Catholics and Protestants as Evidenced by their Symbolic Writings*, Kessinger Legacy Reprints (Whitefish, MT: Kessinger Publishing, 2010), 23–82. Cf. Church of Scotland, *Confession of Faith of the Assembly of Divines at Westminster* (London: The Banner of Truth Trust, 2020), 33–38.

92   Isaiah 57:15: God "inhabits eternity." (RSV-2CE)

93   "To God, all moments are present in their immediacy." *Catechism of the Catholic Church*, 600.

94   *Catechism of the Catholic Church*, 645.

95   *Catechism of the Catholic Church*, 646.

96   (RSV-2CE)

97   (RSV-2CE)

98   (NRSV-CE)

99   (RSV-2CE)

100 (NABRE)

101 (RSV-2CE)

102 Exodus 34:30 (RSV-2CE)

103 Genesis 1:31: "And God saw everything that he had made, and behold, it was very good." (RSV-2CE)

104 Ratzinger, *Eschatology: Death and Eternal Life*, 107.

105 (RSV-2CE) In the Bible, to be at the right hand "is to be identified as being in the special place of honor." Eds. Leland Rykeb, James Wilhoit, and Tremper Longman III, "Right, Right Hand," Dictionary of Biblical Imagery (Westmont, IL: InterVarsity Press, 1998), 727–28.

106 "The unique and altogether singular event of the Incarnation of the Son of God does not mean that Jesus Christ is part God and part man, nor does it imply that he is the result of a confused mixture of the divine and the human. He became truly man while remaining truly God. Jesus Christ is true God and true man." *Catechism of the Catholic Church*, 464. Cf. *Catechism of the Catholic Church*, 467, 503.

107 Matthew 3:17 (RSV-2CE)

108 John 3:16 (RSV-2CE)

109 (RSV-2CE)

110 (RSV-2CE)

111 "Those in whom the Spirit dwells are divinized." *Catechism of the Catholic Church*, 1988.

112 (RSV-2CE)

113 (RSV-2CE)

114 *Catechism of the Catholic Church*, 260.

115 Plato, *Timaeus*, trans. Benjamin Jowett, in *The Collected Dialogues*, eds. Edith Hamilton and Huntington Cairns (Bollingen Series LXXI) (Princeton: Princeton University Press, 1961), 29d–e.

116 Many people dismiss the Bible's accounts of timeless existence as fiction, thinking these accounts impossible simply because they describe a state of being that is outside of their lived experience. This mindset is akin to a person who has been deaf from birth insisting

that sound cannot possibly be real merely because he has never heard it.

117 Man "alone is called to share, by knowledge and love, in God's own life. It was for this end that he was created." *Catechism of the Catholic Church*, 356. Redeemed humanity is meant to "become sharers in the divine nature." *Catechism of the Catholic Church*, 51.

118 (RSV-2CE)

119 The reordering of matter entailed the entire material cosmos transforming into a mirror of man's indifference toward God at the moment of the fall. Consequently, all matter in the universe became indifferent to the will of man, henceforth following blind laws of physics. Once matter became indifferent to the will of man, Adam and Eve lost the capacity to reverse the effects of their sin on the material order. In effect, they trapped themselves by causing the material realm to become indifferent to them.

120 Cf. Wisdom 2:23: "God created man...in the image of his own eternity." (RSV-2CE)

121 Genesis 1:26 (RSV-2CE)

122 "On the third day there was a marriage at Cana in Galilee, and the mother of Jesus was there; Jesus also was invited to the marriage, with his disciples. When the wine failed, the mother of Jesus said to him, 'They have no wine.' And Jesus said to her, 'O woman, what have you to do with me? My hour has not yet come.' His mother said to the servants, 'Do whatever he tells you.' Now six stone jars were standing there, for the Jewish rites of purification, each holding twenty or thirty gallons. Jesus said to them, 'Fill the jars with water.' And they filled them up to the brim. He said to them, 'Now draw some out, and take it to the steward of the feast.' So they took it. When the steward of the feast tasted the water now become wine, and did not know where it came from (though the servants who had drawn the water knew), the steward of the feast called the bridegroom and said to him, 'Every man serves the good wine first; and when men have drunk freely, then the poor wine; but you have kept the good wine until now.' This, the first of his signs, Jesus did at Cana in Galilee, and manifested his glory; and his disciples believed in him." (RSV-2CE)

123 "One day he got into a boat with his disciples, and he said to them, 'Let us go across to the other side of the lake.' So they set out, and as they sailed he fell asleep. And a storm of wind came down on the lake, and they were filling with water, and were in danger. And they went and woke him, saying, 'Master, Master, we are perishing!' And he awoke and rebuked the wind and the raging waves; and they ceased, and there was a calm. He said to them, 'Where is your faith?' And they were afraid, and they marveled, saying to one another, 'Who then is this, that he commands even wind and water, and they obey him?'" (RSV-2CE)

124 Matthew 14:13–21: "Now when Jesus heard this, he withdrew from there in a boat to a lonely place apart. But when the crowds heard it, they followed him on foot from the towns. As he went ashore he saw a great throng; and he had compassion on them, and healed their sick. When it was evening, the disciples came to him and said, 'This is a lonely place, and the day is now over; send the crowds away to go into the villages and buy food for themselves.' Jesus said, 'They need not go away; you give them something to eat.' They said to him, 'We have only five loaves here and two fish.' And he said, 'Bring them here to me.' Then he ordered the crowds to sit down on the grass; and taking the five loaves and the two fish he looked up to heaven, and blessed, and broke and gave the loaves to the disciples, and the disciples gave them to the crowds. And they all ate and were satisfied. And they took up twelve baskets full of the broken pieces left over. And those who ate were about five thousand men, besides women and children." (RSV-2CE)

125 (RSV-2CE)

126 (NABRE) Jesus made the statement about having faith as small as a mustard seed in the context of his disciples being unable to drive out an evil spirit from a child, but the message of Matthew 17:14–20 can be construed more broadly as a statement of the level of faith needed to restore a child of God to his proper state through the removal of the spirit of evil which resides deep within him. Faith in God as small as a mustard seed is enough for God to remove the evil within a believer, thereby restoring that person to the proper state of being.

127 (RSV-2CE)

128 (RSV-2CE)

129 "And the LORD God commanded the man, saying, 'You may freely eat of every tree of the garden; but of the tree of the knowledge of good and evil you shall not eat, for in the day that you eat of it you shall die.'" (RSV-2CE)

130 Divine revelation is the only way man can acquire insight into the original cause of physical creation itself. Cf. *Catechism of the Catholic Church*, 50–141.

131 (RSV-2CE)

132 (RSV-2CE)

133 Isaiah 57:15: God "inhabits eternity." (RSV-2CE) Wisdom 2:23: "God created man...in the image of his own eternity." (RSV-2CE)

134 In the previous chapter, "evil" was defined as "any willful choice to pursue an objective which can only be acquired or experienced at the expense of love."

135 Just as the soul's separation from the body due to physical injury or ailment represents corporeal death, separation from God due to sin and faithlessness represents spiritual death. The concept of temporal, physical life existing simultaneously with spiritual death is a well-established, orthodox Christian doctrine that is supported by numerous biblical passages. Examples include First Timothy 5:6, which states: "she who is self-indulgent is dead even while she lives." (RSV-2CE) In Luke 9:60 and Matthew 8:22, Christ says to a would-be follower: "leave the dead to bury their own dead." (RSV-2CE) This statement is nonsensical unless Christ is referring to the spiritually dead in the first half of the sentence, and the physically and spiritually dead in the second half of the sentence. Colossians 2:13 states: "And you, who were dead in trespasses..., God made alive together with him." (RSV-2CE) Ephesians 2:1 reads: "you were dead through the trespasses and sins in which you once walked, following the course of this world." (RSV-2CE)

136 *Catechism of the Catholic Church*, 400.

137 Cf. John 17:20–26.

138 Romans 5:12: "sin came into the world through one man and death through sin, and so death spread to all men because all men sinned." (RSV-2CE) Cf. *Catechism of the Catholic Church*, 404: "Adam and Eve committed a *personal* sin, but this sin affected the human nature that they would then transmit *in a fallen state*. It is a sin which will be transmitted by propagation to all mankind, that is, by the transmission of a human nature deprived of original holiness and justice. And that is why original sin is called 'sin' only in an analogical sense: it is a sin 'contracted' and not 'committed'—a state and not an act."

139 First Peter 1:18–19: "You know that you were ransomed from the futile ways inherited from your fathers, not with perishable things such as silver or gold, but with the precious blood of Christ, like that of a lamb without blemish or spot." (RSV-2CE) First Peter 2:22: "He committed no sin, and no deceit was found in his mouth." (NRSV-CE)

140 Cf. Genesis 1:26 and 5:1.

141 Both God and man possess the power to create other beings in their own likeness. Genesis 5:1: "When God created man, he made him in the likeness of God." (RSV-2CE) Genesis 5:3: "When Adam had lived a hundred and thirty years, he become the father of a son in his own likeness, after his image, and named him Seth." (RSV-2CE)

142 *Catechism of the Catholic Church*, 2367. Emphasized language from the original has been deemphasized. Cf. *Catechism of the Catholic Church*, 2371: "human life and the duty of transmitting it are not limited by the horizons of this life only: their true evaluation and full significance can be understood only in reference to *man's eternal destiny*."

143 *Catechism of the Catholic Church*, 307.

144 *Catechism of the Catholic Church*, 1049.

145 "In all his life Jesus presents himself as *our model*. He is 'the perfect man,' who invites us to become his disciples and follow him. In humbling himself, he has given us an example to imitate, through his prayer he draws us to pray, and by his poverty he calls us to accept freely the privations and persecutions that may come our way." *Catechism of the Catholic Church*, 520.

146 "Christ's whole life was lived under the sign of persecution. His own share it with him." *Catechism of the Catholic Church*, 530.

147 (RSV-2CE)

148 God's command to animals and man to "be fruitful and multiply" was given *before* the fall, in Genesis 1:22 and 1:28, respectively. (RSV-2CE)

149 (RSV-2CE)

150 Cf. Ivan Karamazov's powerful speech about the unfair suffering of innocents in "The Grand Inquisitor." Fyodor Mikhaylovich Dostoevsky, *The Brothers Karamazov*, trans. Andrew R. MacAndrew (1880; repr., New York: Bantam Books, 2003), 328–53.

151 Romans 5:12: "sin came into the world through one man and death through sin, and so death spread to all men because all men sinned." (RSV-2CE)

152 (RSV-2CE)

153 The concept of temporal, physical life existing simultaneously with spiritual death is an important tenet of Christianity that appears repeatedly in the Bible. Cf. Colossians 2:13, Ephesians 2:1, First Timothy 5:6, Luke 9:60, and Matthew 8:22.

154 Cf. Romans 5:12.

155 Christ's eternal existence is made clear in John 8:58 when Jesus asserts: "Truly, truly, I say to you, before Abraham was, I am." (RSV-2CE)

156 (RSV-2CE)

157 "From all eternity God chose for the mother of his Son a daughter of Israel, a young Jewish woman of Nazareth in Galilee." *Catechism of the Catholic Church*, 488.

158 *Catechism of the Catholic Church*, 522.

159 Deuteronomy 14:2: "For you are a people holy to the LORD your God, and the LORD has chosen you to be a people for his own possession, out of all the peoples that are on the face of the earth." (RSV-2CE)

160 *Catechism of the Catholic Church*, 522.

161 (RSV-2CE)

162 God announces Jesus "through the mouths of the prophets who succeeded one another in Israel." *Catechism of the Catholic Church*, 522.

163 First Peter 1:18–19: "You know that you were ransomed from the futile ways inherited from your fathers, not with perishable things such as silver or gold, but with the precious blood of Christ, like that of a lamb without blemish or spot." (RSV-2CE) First Peter 2:22: "He committed no sin, and no deceit was found in his mouth." (NRSV-CE)

164 Mark 14:56: "For many bore false witness against him, and their witness did not agree." (RSV-2CE) Cf. Matthew 26:59–63.

165 Cf. Matthew 27:32–37, Mark 15:25, Luke 23:26–38, and John 19:16–30.

166 Matthew 26:27–28: "Then he took a cup, and after giving thanks he gave it to them, saying, 'Drink from it, all of you; for this is my blood of the covenant, which is poured out for many for the forgiveness of sins.'" (NRSV-CE)

167 Cf. Matthew 27:57–60, Mark 15:42–46, Luke 23:50–53, and John 19:38–42.

168 Cf. Matthew 27:38–44, Mark 15:27–28, and Luke 23:32–43.

169 Cf. Matthew 28:1–10, Mark 16, Luke 24:1–43, and John 20:1–29.

170 (RSV-2CE)

171 *Catechism of the Catholic Church*, 430.

172 Joseph Ratzinger (Pope Benedict XVI), *The Infancy Narratives*, trans. Philip J. Whitmore. (New York: Image, 2012), 42. Cf. Francis Brown, *The Brown-Driver-Briggs Hebrew and English Lexicon* (1906; repr., Peabody, MA: Hendrickson, 2020): "Yeshua" in Hebrew is a verbal derivative from "to rescue" or "to deliver."

173 Got Questions Ministries, "What Does Exodus 3:14 Mean?" BibleRef, 2020, https://www.bibleref.com/Exodus/3/Exodus-3-14. html.

174 *Catechism of the Catholic Church*, 432.

175 Second Peter 1:4 (RSV-2CE)

176 First John 4:8: "God is love." (RSV-2CE)

177 First John 4:8 (RSV-2CE)

178 (RSV-2CE)

179 *Catechism of the Catholic Church*, 364. Cf. *Catechism of the Catholic Church*, 432: "Jesus united himself to all men through his Incarnation." Cf. *Catechism of the Catholic Church*, 521: "Christ enables us to *live in him* all that he himself lived, and *he lives it in us.* 'By his Incarnation, he, the Son of God, has in a certain way united himself with each man.'"

180 "Jesus Christ is true God and true man, in the unity of his divine person; for this reason he is the one and only mediator between God and men." *Catechism of the Catholic Church*, 480.

181 (RSV-2CE)

182 (RSV-2CE)

183 (NABRE)

184 "The ultimate purpose of creation is that God 'who is the creator of all things may at last become "all in all," thus simultaneously assuring his own glory and our beatitude.'" *Catechism of the Catholic Church*, 294.

185 (RSV-2CE) Cf. John 15:1–4.

186 (RSV-2CE)

187 (RSV-2CE)

188 (RSV-2CE)

189 *Catechism of the Catholic Church*, 460.

190 *Catechism of the Catholic Church*, 460.

191 *Catechism of the Catholic Church*, 1024.

192 "Believing in Jesus Christ and in the One who sent him for our salvation is necessary for obtaining that salvation." *Catechism of the Catholic Church*, 161.

193 (RSV-2CE)

194 (RSV-2CE)

195 "St. Paul speaks of the 'obedience of faith' as our first obligation." *Catechism of the Catholic Church*, 2087.

196 (RSV-2CE)

197 (RSV-2CE)

198 (RSV-2CE)

199 (RSV-2CE)

200 *Catechism of the Catholic Church*, 1033.

201 *Catechism of the Catholic Church*, 1057.

202 *Catechism of the Catholic Church*, 393.

203 *Catechism of the Catholic Church*, 374: "The first man was not only
created good, but was also established in friendship with his Creator
and in harmony with himself and with the creation around him, in a
state that would be surpassed only by the glory of the new creation in
Christ."

204 (RSV-2CE)

205 Because Adam and Eve lacked knowledge of good and evil at the
point when they first committed sin, their sin can be forgiven.

206 Second Peter 2:4: "For if God did not spare the angels when they
sinned, but cast them to hell and committed them to pits of deepest darkness to be kept until the judgment." (RSV-2CE) "There is
no repentance for the angels after their fall." *Catechism of the Catholic
Church*, 393.

207 "How you are fallen from heaven, O Day Star, son of Dawn! How
you are cut down to the ground, you who laid the nations low! You
said in your heart, 'I will ascend to heaven; above the stars of God I
will set my throne on high; I will sit on the mount of assembly in the
far north; I will ascend above the heights of the clouds, I will make
myself like the Most High.'" (RSV-2CE)

208 "And the angels that did not keep their own position but left
their proper dwelling have been kept by him in eternal chains in the
deepest darkness until the judgment of the great day." (RSV-2CE)

209 (RSV-2CE)

210 Michael D. Coogan, Marc Brettler, et al., ed. *The New Oxford Annotated Bible, New Revised Standard Version: An Ecumenical Study Guide, Fifth Edition* (Oxford: Oxford University Press, 2018), 12–13.

211 First John 4:16 (RSV-2CE)

212 This is part of the so-called "problem of divine hiddenness," which involves the issue of whether it is reasonable to believe in God in light of the ambiguity of evidence for God's existence. For more on this topic see, Klaas J. Kraay, "The Problem of Divine Hiddenness," *Oxford Bibliographies*, November 27, 2013, https://www.oxfordbibliographies.com.

213 In Matthew 10:28, Jesus states unequivocally that man has a soul: "And do not fear those who kill the body but cannot kill the soul; rather fear him who can destroy both soul and body in hell." (RSV-2CE)

214 "The Church teaches that every spiritual soul is created immediately by God—it is not 'produced' by the parents—and also that it is immortal: it does not perish when it separates from the body at death." *Catechism of the Catholic Church*, 366. Cf. *Catechism of the Catholic Church*, 33: "The soul, the 'seed of eternity we bear in ourselves, irreducible to the merely material,' can have its origin only in God."

215 *Catechism of the Catholic Church*, 1024.

216 Hebrews 11:6: "And without faith it is impossible to please him." (RSV-2CE). John 3:18: "He who believes in him is not condemned; he who does not believe is condemned already." (RSV-2CE)

217 (NRSV-CE)

218 Isaiah 57:15: God "inhabits eternity." (RSV-2CE) Wisdom 2:23: "God created man...in the image of his own eternity." (RSV-2CE)

219 The initiative lies with the individual to exercise faith. Love would not result were God to somehow exercise faith on behalf of a person because such an act would constitute the usurpation of that person's free will. Because a freely made choice to exercise faith in God is required in order to experience love with God, it is the individual's faith that determines whether he or she will ultimately be healed from the damaging effects of sin and made whole through

unification to God in love. See Christ's statement in Matthew 9:22 and Mark 5:34: *"your* faith has made you well." (RSV-2CE) [Emphasis added.]

220 "Love is patient and kind; love is not jealous or boastful; it is not arrogant or rude. Love does not insist on its own way; it is not irritable or resentful; it does not rejoice at wrong, but rejoices in the right. Love bears all things, believes all things, hopes all things, endures all things." (RSV-2CE)

221 (NABRE)

222 First Corinthians 3:13–15: "each man's work will become manifest; for the Day will disclose it, because it will be revealed with fire, and the fire will test what sort of work each one has done." (RSV-2CE) Cf. Matthew 6:2, which states that seemingly charitable works that are in fact carried out for the purpose of receiving the adulation of men are sinful acts, even though the works themselves may benefit others.

223 (RSV-2CE)

224 Malachi 4:1 (RSV-2CE)

225 Left without even the tiniest root of faith that is "grafted" to the main "root" (the main root being an analogy for God in Romans 11:11–31), left without even the smallest branch that attaches to the "vine" (the vine being an analogy for Christ in John 15:1–11), the faithless will remain forever unable to join to God in love. (RSV-2CE)

226 "The sons of the kingdom [of darkness] will be thrown into the outer darkness; there men will weep and gnash their teeth." (RSV-2CE) Cf. Matthew 22:13: "Then the king said to the attendants, 'Bind him hand and foot, and cast him into the outer darkness, where there will be weeping and gnashing of teeth.'" (RSV-2CE) Cf. Matthew 25:30: "And cast the worthless servant into the outer darkness, where there will be weeping and gnashing of teeth." (RSV-2CE)

227 (RSV-2CE)

228 (RSV-2CE)

229 (RSV-2CE)

230 Cf. Revelation 19:20, 20:10, 20:14–15, and 21:8. (RSV-2CE)

231 Isaiah 57:15: God "inhabits eternity." (RSV-2CE)

232 Wisdom 2:23: "God created man...in the image of his own eternity." (RSV-2CE)

233 (RSV-2CE)

234 Cf. Psalm 90:4: "For a thousand years in your sight are but as yesterday when it is past, or as a watch in the night." (RSV-2CE) Cf. Second Peter 3:8: "But do not ignore this one fact, beloved, that with the Lord one day is as a thousand years, and a thousand years as one day." (RSV-2CE)

235 *Catechism of the Catholic Church*, 600.

236 Proverbs 26:26: "Though his hatred be covered in guile, his wickedness will be uncovered in the assembly." (RSV-2CE) Matthew 10:26: "So have no fear of them; for nothing is covered that will not be revealed, or hidden that will not be known." (RSV-2CE) Mark 4:22: "For there is nothing hidden, except to be made manifest; nor is anything secret, except to come to light." (RSV-2CE) Luke 8:17: "For nothing is hidden that shall not be made manifest, nor anything secret that shall not be known and come to light." (RSV-2CE) Luke 12:3: "Whatever you have said in the dark shall be heard in the light, and what you have whispered in private rooms shall be proclaimed upon the housetops." (RSV-2CE) First Corinthians 4:5: "Therefore do not pronounce judgment before the time, before the Lord comes, who will bring to light the things now hidden in darkness and will disclose the purposes of the heart." (RSV-2CE)

237 (RSV-2CE)

238 (RSV-2CE)

239 (RSV-2CE)

240 (RSV-2CE)

241 Luke 13:30 (RSV-2CE)

242 Matthew 6:20-21 (RSV-2CE)

243 Matthew 25:29 (NABRE)

244 (RSV-2CE)

245 (NRSV-CE)

246 (NRSV-CE)

247 (RSV-2CE)

248 (RSV-2CE)

249 Revelation 21:4: "[God] will wipe away every tear from their eyes, and death shall be no more, neither shall there be mourning nor crying nor pain any more, for the former things have passed away." (RSV-2CE)

250 Genesis 1:26–28 (RSV-2CE)

251 Isaiah 11:6–9 (RSV-2CE)

252 Lewis, *The Problem of Pain*, 22.

253 (NABRE)

254 (RSV-2CE)

255 Isaiah 1:31: "The strong shall become like tinder, and their work like a spark; they and their work shall burn together, with no one to quench them." (NRSV-CE) Malachi 4:1: "For behold, the day comes, burning like an oven, when all the arrogant and all evildoers will be stubble; the day that comes shall burn them up, says the LORD of hosts, so that it will leave them neither root nor branch." (RSV-2CE) Matthew 13:40: "Just as the weeds are gathered and burned with fire, so will it be at the close of the age." (NRSV-CE) John 15:6: "Whoever does not abide in me is thrown away like a branch and withers; such branches are gathered, thrown into the fire, and burned." (NRSV-CE) Revelation 21:8: "But as for the cowardly, the faithless, the polluted, as for murderers, fornicators, sorcerers, idolaters, and all liars, their lot shall be in the lake that burns with fire and brimstone, which is the second death." (RSV-2CE)

256 If the existence of an eternal hell and the destruction of the entire space-time cosmos do not logically conflict with God's all-just and all-loving nature, then the scenes of largescale death and destruction that are described in various Old Testament passages likewise do not logically conflict with God's all-just and all-loving nature. Because every human being is sinful (except Christ), and because death is the just penalty of sin, everyone must suffer this penalty at some point or another. The fact that some people experience this

penalty as part of a largescale destructive event does not in any way establish that God is unjust or unloving.

257 Romans 6:23: "For the wages of sin is death." (RSV-2CE)

258 Psalm 36:9: "For with you is the fountain of life." (RSV-2CE)

259 Just as the soul's separation from the body due to physical injury or ailment represents corporeal death, the soul's separation from God due to sin represents spiritual death. Cf. Colossians 2:13, Ephesians 2:1, First Timothy 5:6, Luke 9:60, and Matthew 8:22.

260 (RSV-2CE)

261 Cf. Romans 11:22: "Note then the kindness and the severity of God: severity toward those who have fallen, but kindness to you, provided you continue in his kindness; otherwise you too will be cut off." (RSV-2CE)

262 Revelation 21:4 (RSV-2CE)

263 Isaiah 66:24 (RSV-2CE) The essence of sin is that it is opposed to love. Since God is love itself, those who give themselves over to sin are enemies of God, who have "rebelled against" him.

264 The hideousness of sin in the eyes of a perfectly sinless being explains why God takes such an uncompromising stance toward sin in the Bible. Readers of the Bible who do not grasp the utterly repulsive nature of sin often view God's uncompromising stance toward sin as a cruelty, when in fact, God's stance toward sin is wholly just.

265 (RSV-2CE)

266 As a reminder, the fifth prerequisite of love requires individuals in a loving relationship to abstain from the pursuit of self-centered ends that can only be obtained at the expense of another person in the relationship. This requires the courage to risk at least some form of personal loss if one is wrong about placing faith in another person. All loving relationships work in this manner.

267 Isaiah 11:6–9: "the earth shall be full of the knowledge of the Lord as the waters cover the sea." (RSV-2CE)

268 Revelation 7:14–15: "These are they who have come out of the great tribulation; they have washed their robes and made them white

in the blood of the Lamb. Therefore are they before the throne of God, and serve him day and night within his temple; and he who sits upon the throne will shelter them with his presence." (RSV-2CE)

269 Revelation 7:9 (RSV-2CE)

270 First Corinthians 12 (RSV-2CE)

271 "Those in whom the Spirit dwells are divinized." *Catechism of the Catholic Church*, 1988. "The ultimate end of the whole divine economy is the entry of God's creatures into the perfect unity of the Blessed Trinity." *Catechism of the Catholic Church*, 260. Second Peter 1:4 states that through Christ redeemed man becomes "partakers of the divine nature." (RSV-2CE)

272 Malachi 4:2: "You shall go forth leaping like calves from the stall." (RSV-2CE)

273 The argument that God's grace is not needed for salvation is a heresy known as "Pelagianism." God's grace is required for salvation because, following the fall, every person is brought into existence in a sinful state of being. Man does not have the capacity to remove his sin nature through his own efforts. Only God can restore fallen man to the proper state of being.

274 Romans 11:6: "But if it is by grace, it is no longer on the basis of works; otherwise grace would no longer be grace." (RSV-2CE) Ephesians 2:8–9: "For by grace you have been saved through faith; and this is not your own doing, it is the gift of God—not because of works, lest any man should boast." (RSV-2CE) Titus 3:5: "he saved us, not because of deeds done by us in righteousness, but in virtue of his own mercy, by the washing of regeneration and renewal in the Holy Spirit." (RSV-2CE)

275 (RSV-2CE)

276 Matthew 7:15–19 (RSV-2CE)

277 Matthew 7:20 (RSV-2CE)

278 (RSV-2CE)

279 This view aligns with the Catholic doctrine that genuine faith will always be accompanied by good works of some kind, even if those works consist of nothing more than refraining from engaging

in certain wrongful actions that the person would have committed otherwise. The only exceptions are when believers do not have opportunity to engage in good works.

280 Cf. Matthew 24:22 and 24:31, Luke 18:7, Romans 8:33, Second Timothy 2:10, Titus 1:1, and Second Peter 1:10. (RSV-2CE)

281 John Calvin's writings on predestination provide a more detailed examination of this doctrine.

282 (RSV-2CE)

283 *Catechism of the Catholic Church*, 600.

284 *Catechism of the Catholic Church*, 1037.

285 Robert Sapolsky, *Determined: A Science of Life Without Free Will* (New York: Penguin Press, 2023), Chapter 10.5.

286 Timothy Revell, "Why Free Will Doesn't Exist, according to Robert Sapolsky," *New Scientist*, "CultureLab" podcast, October 18, 2023. https://www.newscientist.com/article/2398369-why-free-will-doesnt-exist-according-to-robert-sapolsky/.

287 Sean Illing, "What our brain chemistry says about free will: In his new book, Stanford professor Robert Sapolsky argues that free will is a myth." *Vox*, "The Gray Area" podcast, November 21, 2023. https://www.vox.com/the-gray-area/23965798/free-will-robert-sapolsky-determined-the-gray-area.

288 (RSV-2CE)

289 Matthew 13:11 (RSV-2CE)

290 *Catechism of the Catholic Church*, 546.

291 Cf. Hebrews 11:6: "And without faith it is impossible to please him. For whoever would draw near to God must believe that he exists and that he rewards those who seek him." (RSV-2CE)

292 (NRSV-CE)

293 (RSV-2CE)

294 (RSV-2CE)

295 "How you are fallen from heaven, O Day Star, son of Dawn! How you are cut down to the ground, you who laid the nations low! You

said in your heart, 'I will ascend to heaven; above the stars of God I will set my throne on high; I will sit on the mount of assembly in the far north; I will ascend above the heights of the clouds, I will make myself like the Most High.'" (RSV-2CE)

296 This may explain why Sapolsky described this moment as an "existentially unnerving experience." It appears to have been the moment when he decisively rejected God.

297 For a discussion on this topic, see Leszek Kolakowski, *Why Is There Something Rather than Nothing?*, trans. Agnieszka Kolakowska (2004; repr., New York: Basic Books, 2007).

298 "In many ways, throughout history down to the present day, men have given expression to their quest for God in their religious beliefs and behavior: in their prayers, sacrifices, rituals, meditations, and so forth. These forms of religious expression, despite the ambiguities they often bring with them, are so universal that one may well call man a *religious being.*" *Catechism of the Catholic Church*, 28.

299 "With his openness to truth and beauty, his sense of moral goodness, his freedom and the voice of his conscious, with his longings for the infinite and for happiness, man questions himself about God's existence." *Catechism of the Catholic Church*, 33.

300 "'Where do we come from?' 'Where are we going?' 'What is our origin?' 'What is our end?' 'Where does everything that exists come from and where is it going?' The two questions, the first about the origin and the second about the end, are inseparable. They are decisive for the meaning and orientation of our life and actions." *Catechism of the Catholic Church*, 282.

301 "Human intelligence is surely already capable of finding a response to the question of origins." *Catechism of the Catholic Church*, 286. "But this search for God demands of man every effort of intellect, a sound will, 'an upright heart,' as well as the witness of others who teach him to seek God." *Catechism of the Catholic Church*, 30.

302 Matthew 22:34–40 and Mark 12:28–24 state that love is the greatest of all God's commandments. First Corinthians 12:12–26 states that redeemed man will become "one body" with God. (RSV-2CE) Second Peter 1:4 states that through Christ redeemed man becomes

"partakers of the divine nature." (RSV-2CE) Together, these and similar passages communicate that the ultimate purpose of man's creation is to be joined to God in love.

303 *Catechism of the Catholic Church*, 68.

304 Cf. Luke 13:1–5: "There were some present at that very time who told him of the Galileans whose blood Pilate had mingled with their sacrifices. And he answered them, 'Do you think that these Galileans were worse sinners than all the other Galileans, because they suffered thus? I tell you, No; but unless you repent you will all likewise perish. Or those eighteen upon whom the tower in Siloam fell and killed them, do you think that they were worse offenders than all the others who dwelt in Jerusalem? I tell you, No; but unless you repent you will all likewise perish.'" (RSV-2CE)

305 Ratzinger, *The Infancy Narratives*, 43–44.

306 Ratzinger, *The Infancy Narratives*, 44.

307 Genesis 1:26 (RSV-2CE)

308 Genesis 1:26 (RSV-2CE)

309 Contrast this with a system in which every life form acts selflessly, to the benefit of all other life forms. Cf. Isaiah 11:6: "The wolf shall dwell with the lamb, and the leopard shall lie down with the kid, and the calf and the lion and the fatling together, and a little child shall lead them." (RSV-2CE)

310 "The whole human race is in Adam 'as one body of one man.' By this 'unity of the human race' all men are implicated in Adam's sin, as all are implicated in Christ's justice." *Catechism of the Catholic Church*, 404; Cf. *Catechism of the Catholic Church*, 790–91.

311 "God has no other reason for creating than his love and goodness." *Catechism of the Catholic Church*, 293.

312 G. W. Leibniz, *Theodicy: Essays on the Goodness of God, the Freedom of Man, and the Origin of Evil*, trans. E. M. Huggard (Chicago: Open Court, 1985), 53–9, 105–7, 126–29, 134–37.

313 (RSV-2CE)

314 "The ultimate end of the whole divine economy is the entry of God's creatures into the perfect unity of the Blessed Trinity." *Catechism of the Catholic Church*, 260; Cf. *Catechism of the Catholic Church*, 781–98.

315 "Only in the knowledge of God's plan for man can we grasp that sin is an abuse of the freedom that God gives to created persons so that they are capable of loving him and loving one another." *Catechism of the Catholic Church*, 387.

316 "It pleased God, in his goodness and wisdom, to reveal himself and to make known the mystery of his will. His will was that men should have access to the Father, through Christ, the Word made flesh, in the Holy Spirit, and thus become sharers in the divine nature." *Catechism of the Catholic Church*, 51; Cf. *Catechism of the Catholic Church*, 68: "By love, God has revealed himself and given himself to man. He has thus provided the definitive, superabundant answer to the questions that man asks himself about the meaning and purpose of his life."

317 Jeremiah 20:12 (RSV-2CE)

318 (NABRE)

319 Romans 8:32 (RSV-2CE)

320 Second Corinthians 5:21: "For our sake he made him to be sin who knew no sin, so that in him we might become the righteousness of God." (RSV-2CE)

321 (RSV-2CE)

322 Weil, "Forms of the Implicit Love of God," 74–5.

323 "The Church has never forgotten that 'sinners were the authors and the ministers of all the sufferings that the divine Redeemer endured.'" *Catechism of the Catholic Church*, 598.

324 "God's love is stronger than death." *Catechism of the Catholic Church*, 1040.

325 Second Thessalonians 1:10: "When he comes on that day to be glorified in his saints, and to be marveled at in all who have believed." (RSV-2CE)

326 Weil, "Forms of the Implicit Love of God," 74.

327 Matthew 22:34–40

328 Psalm 119:75: "I know, O Lᴏʀᴅ, that your judgments are right, and that in faithfulness you have afflicted me." (RSV-2CE)

329 Job contains one of the most frequently cited discussions of suffering in the Bible. However, it does not provide the solution to the problem of pain, which is why it is not a focus of this book. The solution to the problem of pain centers on Genesis 1–3 and the life and teachings of Jesus Christ.

330 Cf. Wisdom 2.

331 "The whole of man's history has been the story of dour combat with the powers of evil, stretching, so our Lord tells us, from the very dawn of history until the last day. Finding himself in the midst of the battlefield man has to struggle to do what is right, and it is at great cost to himself, and aided by God's grace, that he succeeds in achieving his own inner integrity." *Catechism of the Catholic Church*, 409. Cf. *Catechism of the Catholic Church*, 2520–27.

332 Matthew 18:3: "Truly, I say to you, unless you turn and become like children, you will never enter the kingdom of heaven." (RSV-2CE) Simple, childlike faith is a precondition of experiencing relational love with God. Since salvation consists of entering into a timeless loving relationship with God, faith in God as unadulterated and simple as that of a child is needed for salvation.

333 *Catechism of the Catholic Church*, 1723.

334 Matthew 6:23: "But if your eye is not sound, your whole body will be full of darkness. If then the light in you is darkness, how great is the darkness!" (RSV-2CE)

335 The snares of materialism are famously described in First Timothy 6:10: "For the love of money is a root of all kinds of evil, and in their eagerness to be rich some have wandered away from the faith and pierced themselves with many pains." (NRSV-CE)

336 *Catechism of the Catholic Church*, 1723.

337 *Catechism of the Catholic Church*, 1718.

338 *Catechism of the Catholic Church*, 1718. Cf. *Catechism of the Catholic Church*, 27: "The desire for God is written in the human heart, because man is created by God and for God; and God never ceases to draw man to himself. Only in God will he find the truth and happiness he never stops searching for."

339 God "never ceases to call every man to seek him, so as to find life and happiness." *Catechism of the Catholic Church*, 30.

340 Søren Kierkegaard, *Works of Love*, trans. Howard and Edna Hong (1847; repr., New York: Harper & Row, 1962), 23–24.

Made in the USA
Columbia, SC
29 August 2024

bf193593-68bb-4efa-9cd8-00027547a3e3R01